MOUNTAIN LAKE RESORT

BOOK I

1751 - 1900

Other Books by the Author

James Patton and the Appalachian Colonists

William Preston and the Allegheny Patriots

General Andrew Lewis of Roanoke and Greenbrier

Elder Jacob Miller Founder of Dunkard Churches
Virginia, Ohio and Indiana and Descendants

The New River Early Settlement

Springfield Saga The Thompsons of Fort Thompson on
New River, Pulaski County, Virginia

The United States Army Invades the New River Valley
May 1864

Books Published by the Author

History and Membership of Gravel Hill Christian
Church 1830

James B. Price General Store Price's Fork Account
Book 1871

Mountain Lake Resort

By

Patricia Givens Johnson

Mountain Lake Resort
Book I
1751-1900

ISBN Number 0-9614765-8-3

Library of Congress Catalog Card Number - 87-51181

Dedicated to

Kara and Lindsay

Who Love the Mountain Lake Ducks

Contents

Mountain Lake as Christopher Gist first saw it in 1751 (Photo courtesy of Gilbert Porterfield)

Introduction

Mountain Lake, Giles County, Virginia, has been called "The Silver Gem of the Alleghenies". It has an elevation of 3874 feet. Bald Knob rising behind the lake has an elevation of 4327 feet. Virginia Geological Survey soundings show that the head of the lake is shallow and it gradually increases to a depth of 100 feet. This greatest depth was discovered about 75 yards from the outlet and it decreases rapidly until the outlet is reached. This depth may vary as the lake increases in size. The water level dramatically changes over the years. Geologists can show that the lake has fluctuated from around one hundred feet to about thirty in depth. At about eighty feet in depth when Gist discovered it, the lake went down to a small pond from 1768-1804. By 1820 it was half full. In 1835 it was full but just after the Civil War about 1869 it had gone back to a small pond with trees growing in the basin. By 1871 it had returned to lake size and remained so until the present with milder fluctuations in depth during dry seasons. Though dead tree trunks are on the lake's bottom they have not been found below 30 feet which indicates the lake has never gone much below that level.

Mountain Lake is the only natural lake in the unglaciated southern Appalachians. It is drained by Salt Pond Drain which follows a north-northwesternly course until it joins Little Stony Creek.

Mountain Lake is believed by geologists to have been formed by rock slides and damming. The depression now occupied by Mountain Lake possibly resulted from the breaching of an open, northeast-plunging anticline. Erosion by Salt Pond Drain which flows north has been slow because of resistant sandstones which overlie the easily eroded Martinsburg Shale now in place at the south end of the lake and near the head of Doe Creek. A impressive valley has been formed by Doe Creek which failed by very little to reach and drain Mountain Lake. Doe Creek may be related to an older New River erosion surface. Today large Tuscarora blocks form a colluvial dam where Salt Pond Drain leaves the lake basin. Damming may have been gradual or sudden. While the ice sheets to the north were retreating snow and ice would continue to cover mountains in the area. In this period freeze-thaw cycles would be common to Mountain Lake and large blocks of Tuscarora may have begun the damming process following the close of the Pleistocene Epoch, 7000 to 9000 years ago or even as early as the last Ice Age. The possibility exists that one or more catastrophic events may have caused the damming. Records of earthquakes in recent times reveal that the area is one of considerable activity. Scientists conclude today that Mountain Lake was formed by damming and that major earthquake activity today could alter the level of the lake dramatically.

Geographically Mountain Lake situated on Salt Pond Mountain is located on the divide between the Atlantic and Mississippi watershed. Waters from Salt Pond Drain find their way to the Mississippi by way of New River. John's Creek rising directly under Bald Knob flows east into the James and thence to the Atlantic.

Mountain Lake may be reached by two roads leading from U.S. 460. One, Virginia 700, about two miles northwest of Newport crosses Sinking Creek over a new bridge near the Mountain Lake sign. Nearby is the old red covered bridge, built in 1912, which is one of the few remaining covered bridges of Virginia. The other road leaves U.S. 460 at Hoge's Chapel, one mile southeast of Pembroke and goes up the Doe Creek Valley. Known as the Doe Creek Road it once was the main road up the mountain.

CHAPTER 1

Christopher Gist Discovers Mountain Lake

The first white man to record that he had seen Mountain Lake was the explorer Christopher Gist. Several years later he would save George Washington's life when he made his famous trip to the Ohio French forts.

Gist was sent by the Ohio Land Company in October 1750 on a land hunting expedition in the Ohio and Kanawha drainage basin. Gist was a likely candidate for the job. A descendant of Oliver Cromwell, Lord Protector of England, Gist's father Richard, Captain Surveyor of Maryland, had surveyed the town of Baltimore. Gist's mother was descended from the mountain loving Scottish dukes of Athole. Gist himself had recently settled near present Wilkesboro, North Carolina. At the top of the mountains nearby were the headwaters of New River which fed the Ohio. Gist had probably already explored on New River before he spent the winter exploring on the Ohio. On his way home in the spring of 1751 he followed New River back to Virginia.

Saturday, May 11, found him on Big Stony Creek and near Sinking Creek in present Giles County. He says he came to a creek and meadow where "we let our horses feed, then (traveled) SE 2 M, S 1 M, SE 2 M to a very high Mountain on the top of which was a Lake or Pond about 3/4 of a mile long NE & SW and 1/4 of a mile wide, the water fresh and clear, and a clean gravelly shore about 10 yds wide with a fine meadow and six fine springs in it."

This first description of Mountain Lake he wrote in a journal later sent to the Ohio Company which was avidly read by land speculators in London. Soon after discovery it was known in England that there was such a place as Mountain Lake in the Allegheny Mountains of Virginia.

Within a few years Gist was given another job. This time the Virginia government had him accompany George Washington to the Ohio Valley to order the French to leave the forts they were building there. On this trip Gist saved Washington's life twice, once from an Indian arrow and again from drowning in the Ohio River when he fell in the raging current. Gist would live through Braddock's defeat, and through the French and Indian War only to be felled by smallpox in 1759.

The French and Indian War from 1754 to 1763 was followed by Pontiac's War in 1763 which lasted until 1765 driving out of the New River Valley those hardy few that had come after Gist. Only about 1766 did people began to venture back in the vicinity of Mountain Lake.

John Lybrook's family had settled before 1750 on Little Stony and Doe creeks which drained Mountain Lake mountain and they were now back expanding their settlement. The Burks and Snidows (Snydows) built a fort near where Doe Creek enters the New. All these families explored Mountain Lake.

In 1768 John Chapman from Culpepper County, Virginia, arrived at the mouth of Walker's Creek on the New and built his cabin. His son Henley would later own Mountain Lake. Some say John Chapman was actually the first owner of Mountain Lake. In the coming years Chapman busily cleared a settlement and served in Dunmore's War and the American Revolution. He had little time for a lake even if he did own it.

The same year, 1768, that John Chapman arrived on New River a drought was beginning. Geologists say that from 1768 to 1804 a drought nearly dried up the lake.

It is apparent that during the Revolution the lake receded drastically from the size Christopher Gist had seen.

Colonel Christian Snidow recalled in 1836 that he could remember it from 1776 and that the lake had not increased in length but had risen. Col. Snidow informed Valley of Virginia historian Samuel Kercheval that when the lake "was first known to the white people, vast numbers of buffaloes, elks and deer resorted to it, and drank freely of its waters; from which circumstances it acquired the name 'Salt Pond'."

Scientists say that in the dry period during the Revolution trees grew up where the bed had once been.

It is easy to see how the lake diminished in size. During the drought period large flocks of wild animals in the mountains would naturally flock to its banks seeking water. If the drought lasted long enough the springs that fed it would dry up. Large herds constantly drinking with no replacement of water would make the lake diminish. Settlers throughout the mountains would also drive their flocks there to drink. At the same time they would throw out salt for their herds. There were also salt or mineral rocks present that the animals licked even before the white man came.

In the mid-1800's the author's great-grandfather Andrew Williams drove his cattle from present Maybrook up to the "Salt Pond" to salt them. The expression "Salt Pond" simply came from salt thrown out by men feeding cattle. So Gist's Mountain Lake actually fed by springs of pure water became "the Salt Pond".

When the drought ended settlers did not have to come as often to the Salt Pond and it was during this period with out so many herds trampling around that brush began to cover the receded bed. In one season in the Alleghenies a body of neglected yet fertile land can grow to over a man's head with new growth of saplings which the next season begin to grow into trees. If the lake nearly dried up to little more than a pond overgrown with trees and underbrush during this period most people would have believed it was a lake that came and went.

During the Revolutionary period Mountain Lake became a hiding place for outlaws. The mountains of Giles County were noted as hide-outs for Tories and deserters from both the British and American armies. Mountain Lake was an ideal hide-out. There were springs of pure water and natural salt-bearing rocks which the herds licked. An abundant supply of buffalo and deer was readily available.The inaccessible region added to its attraction for those who had placed themselves beyond the law.

After the Revolution a man named Samuel McGraw became the owner of Mountain Lake. He was the owner on 29 January 1789 of a tract "lying in Montgomery County on Salt Pond Mountain including the pond and the heads of Little Stony and John's Creek". McGraw's name labels him as Scotch or Scotch-Irish a race noted for ingenuity and enterprise. McGraw possessed the lake during the drought and may have charged a toll from the local farmers for watering herds. When it began to rain again and farmers did not come so frequently he may have found that a pond on top of an inaccessible mountain was a bad deal. Whatever his reason McGraw sold. Ownership was transferred on July 5, 1794 to William Price. In the package Price bought "1000 acres including the pond". The survey was made by Gordon Cloyd, Montgomery County Surveyor, assisted by chain carriers David Lucas and Sherod Atkins.

A man named Sherod Atkins had been a Tory in Pittsylvania County. Whether the same man was the Mountain Lake chain carrier is unknown but probably was.The Atkins family have a legend that the Tory Sherod was the son of Jacob Harley a British tax-collector who was the son of the Earl of Oxford. If Sherod was the grandson of a British Earl it explains why he fled from the patriots (who had sent a file of men to capture him) and found his way to the vicinity of Salt Pond Mountain.

There were a number of men named David Lucas in the area. A David Lucas murdered a man and was hanged at Giles Courthouse on June 24, 1842. The executed David Lucas had a brother Jeremiah Lucas who had also killed a man during the War of 1812. Jeremiah, fleeing justice, had hid out on Salt Pond Mountain. Mountain Lake folk today say that the criminal Dave Lucas and his brother Jeremiah both hung around the upper reaches of Doe Creek and the lake. It seems that the Mountain Lake area for a time was frequented by men beyond the law.

By 1794 a trail had been beaten out up to the lake. Now the lake was accessible to any horseman - outlaw or otherwise.

We can tell from Gordon Cloyd'survey that the body of water during this period was called Salt Pond and the mountain took its name from the name of the pond or lake.

In 1805 when Giles County was formed from Montgomery County Mountain Lake fell in the bounds of Giles. The water had begun to rise again. Edward Pollard writing in his travel guide, "The Virginia Tourist" in 1869 says that the lake "was said to have been forming, gradually enlarging for more than sixty years,its first appearance noticed in 1804."

The next development in Mountain Lake's history was its purchase by an influential man.

Henley Chapman was the first Commonwealth's Attorney for Giles and a member of the Convention that framed Virginia's Constitution in 1829. Living on New River at the mouth of Walker's Creek Henley knew of the natural features in the vicinity. He saw a potential in the old Gunpowder Springs of Adam Harman at present Eggleston so would eventually buy them and begin a resort called Chapman's Springs. He knew of the Mountain Lake high up on Salt Pond and saw some potential there also. He bought the lake and the surrounding tract of land early in the 1800's. Years later Henley Chapman told William C. Pendleton a historian that he owned "the place where Mountain Lake is and ranged his cattle, as did other settlers, on the mountain thereabout; and that he and others used the basin as a salting ground for their cattle. He said that the trees seen (growing in the lake's bottom) were there, alive and full of foliage in the summer time, when he salted his cattle in the basin, and before the water began to accumulate in a body."

John Lybrook and Christian Snidow who lived on Doe Creek and Little Stony, which drain the top of Salt Pond Mountain, also told the historian Samuel Kercheval about the lake. Kercheval said that in 1804 there was a remarkably wet spring and summer and that the pond began to fill up again from that time. "Col. Snydow also informed (Kercheval) that previous to the rising of the water, a very large spring raised at the head and supplied the lake with water; but since its rise, that spring has disappeared, and it is now fed by numerous small springs around its head."

So we have glimpses of what Mountain Lake was like in the 1700's from the first white men who settled near it. These are all the known recorded accounts of the earliest recollections of white men of Mountain Lake and Salt Pond Mountain.

The view from Salt Pond Mountain down into Giles County as seen by naturalist Lyon in 1809
(Author's Collections)

CHAPTER 2

The First Naturalists

By the early 1800's Mountain Lake was widely known not only as an unusual physical phenomena but for the exceptional plants that grew around it.

In 1802 Benjamin Smith Barton a leading botanist in Philadelphia and professor at the University of Pennsylvania made a botanizing trip to Virginia and possibly came to Salt Pond hunting for rare plants. If he did not come in 1802 he came sometime later. Nesta Ewan, formerly of Tulane University, an authority on botany, tells us that Benjamin Smith Barton did visit Salt Pond Mountain.

Four years later Barton sent his protege Frederick Pursch over the same itinerary he had made in 1802. In 1799 Pursch left Dresden, Germany, where he had worked in the Royal Botanic Gardens and came to America to investigate American plantlife. After arrival in Pennsylvania he worked for various wealthy men and met Benjamin Barton. In 1805 Jefferson received plants from Lewis and Clark and turned them over to Barton to catalogue. Barton passed this task on to Pursch. In 1806 "by the kind assistance" of Barton, Pursch botanized from Maryland to Virginia and into present West Virginia. He left Pennsylvania in the spring traveling on foot with only a dog and gun since he believed that "the most attentive way for observation." He visited Natural Bridge, Greenbrier County, Keeneys Knob, Walkers Meadows, New River, Salt Pond Mountain and Christiansburg, then back to Pennsylvania in the autumn of 1806. From what he learned on Salt Pond and other places he put together a book, Flora Americae Septentrionalis.

In August 1809 naturalist John Lyon came from Philadelphia to Giles County, Virginia, with the purpose of searching for unusual plants on Salt Pond Mountain. By August 4 Lyon was at Fincastle and traveled that day to Blacksburg a distance of 41 miles.

On August 5 he traveled through showery weather all day "to Mr. Parker Lucas's on Sinking Creek a distance of 11 miles". On August 6 he went up to the top of Salt Pond Mountain guided by Lucas.

"The mountain," says Lyon, "is one of the highest in Virginia and affords a most extensive prospect. The Pond or Lake is about a mile and a quarter long by half a mile broad to which there is a little descent from the highest summit of the mountain."

Then Lyon makes a very interesting statement.

"Why it has obtained the name of the Salt Pond I cannot learn but the water is quite fresh and clear. It is said to be very deep, conjecture says 150 or 200 feet deep in the middle but I cannot learn that it has ever been accurately measured."

It seems that Parker Lucas could have told Lyon that it got the name Salt Pond from people salting their cattle there as well as something about the origin of the lake if this were so well known. We wonder why he did not.

"There is a number of uncommon plants on this mountain," reported Lyon, "as Cimicifuga palmata (trautuettaria palmata), Saxifraga Leucanthemifolia (parnassia caroliniana), Parnassia caroliniana and many others new to me."

Lyon must have spent two days searching plants on Salt Pond Mountain for on August 7 he left Lucas's, crossed New River at Lybrook's ferry and as he says "got to Montgomery about 32 miles over a rough thinly settled country, roads bad and difficult to find, accomodations very indifferent." By August 8 Lyon was in "Wythe Town."

According to Nesta Ewan wife of Joseph Ewan who edited Lyon's Journal, Benjamin Barton, Frederick Pursch and John Lyon, leading early American naturalists, "all visited Salt Pond Mountain but none left any detailed description of what they found."

CHAPTER 3

Mapmakers Find Mountain Lake

By 1810 due to reports by visitors such as the botanists and Henley Chapman Mountain Lake was becoming well known. Chapman, noted as the "First Citizen of Giles" and in the legislature at Richmond, told about the lake on visits to Richmond. People in the sweltering city and other places would listen as he told of the cool breezes of Giles County and Mountain Lake. Tidewater people must have visualized a Little Switzerland as they listened. Advertisements for the lake also appeared in various Virginia newspapers.

By 1825 Montain Lake was well enough known to be on Herman Boy's "Map of Virginia" which shows the salt pond labeled as "lake" and two roads up to it, the Doe Creek road and a road from the vicinity of Newport - in fact very much the same roads that exist today.

Next Mountain Lake appeared in a gazetteer in 1835. Joseph Martin's "A New and Comprehensive Gazetteer of Virginia and the District of Columbia" features the lake.

It says, "The "Salt Pond" is located five miles from "Hygaen Springs" the fancy name that Adam Harman's Gunpowder Springs or the New River White Sulphur had at this time.

Martin then describes Mountain Lake. He says, "Salt Pond is a natural lake located on the supposed highest mountain in Virginia, an Allegheny Mountain. Daily stages are running from Wythe Court House to Lewisburg through Pearisburg and mail from Franklin and Tazewell once a week." The nearest town was "Parisburg" inhabited by 170 whites, 34 negroes accommodated by one doctor and two lawyers.

The scenery along the New River is grand says Martin mentioning particularly Pompey's Pillar and Caesar's Arch near Hygaen Springs. But it was the Salt Pond that Martin said deserves particular notice.

"This mountain derives its name from the circumstances that the old settlers of the county usually gathered their stock that ran on the range of this place for the purpose of giving them salt. It is an immense lake of unknown depth, 3 or 4 miles in circumference. It is said by the old settlers that this pond has risen from a spring which flowed into a kind of natural basin situated between two lofty mountains... gradually increased overtopping tree after tree until it at last found an outlet over the ridge that unites the two mountains. This pond ... frequently excites the curiosity of strangers and to which the gentry of the county often resort for the object of pleasure and amusement."

Martin mentions mud and blue catfish in New River weighing 60-70 pounds. He says Giles hemp is a particular staple raised near Salt Pond and sold to Buchanan at the head of navigation on the James River.

The author's grandmother Josephine Williams Porterfield remembered as a young girl beating and washing hemp in Sinking Creek just at the foot of Salt Pond Mountain. There is still a "Hemp Hollow" in Newport reminiscent of these times.

CHAPTER 4

Blue Devils and Black Plague

In the 1830's there was a reason for mapmakers and gazetteers to be frantically locating healthful places for tourists.

For years malarial fevers and the dreaded yellow fever had ravaged the southern coastal cities. In 1832 another even more dreaded pestilence arrived in America aboard ships that docked in Norfolk, Charleston and other southern ports. People frantically sought refuge from it.

1832 was called "The Year of the Cholera". In Virginia it broke out in Norfolk. The Negro slaves were the hardest hit. The Negro had a racial innoculation against yellow fever but not against cholera. Soon it was raging in New Orleans. Little was known about how the disease spread. Today we know it was carried by rats on the ships that put into the southern ports from Norfolk to New Orleans. Then it was generally believed that it rose from the low marshy areas of the Tidewater and people thought by fleeing to the mountains they could escape. Various enterprising doctors began to seek good springs in Virginia where people might escape the ravages of this plague and any others that might beset the population.

Dr. Thomas Goode bought Hot Springs while Dr. William Burke of Richmond and Alabama bought the Red Sulphur. Both purchased in 1832.

Prior to this some South Carolinians had taken over Salt Sulphur Springs in Monroe County just over an Allegheny mountain range from Mountain Lake. Under John Legare they made a little colony of South Carolina there. At White Sulphur Springs the South Carolinians began to build cottages for themselves a practice that would spread to Mountain Lake.

In 1834 Philip Nicklin of Philadelphia writing under the pen name of Peregrine Prelix, on a tour of the Virginia Springs, visited Red Sulphur Springs, Grey Sulphur and Salt Sulphur, all just over the mountain from Mountain Lake. He unfortunately did not get to Mountain Lake. His colorful descriptions wherever he went are priceless and he would surely have given some succulent pictures of Mountain Lake had he visited there.

He describes the people visiting the resorts in the 1830's. He said they came to cure "yellow jaundice, white swelling, Blue Devils, Black Plague, Scarlet fever, Yellow fever, Spotted fever, fever of every color, hydrophobia, hypocondria, hypocrisy ... gout, gormandising, grogging, colic, stone, gravel and all diseases and bad habits except chewing, smoking, spitting and swearing."

Nicklin tells us, "We passed the night at the Red Sulphur, and at six the next morning I mounted beside the driver of the Salt Sulphur coach leaving my fellow traveler, who was desirous of visiting Salt Pond on the Allegheny mountain.

"As I did not see Salt Pond with my own eyes, I shall not describe it, only observing that though the pond is salt, yet the water is fresh and that it may be paradoxically considered as one of nature's artificial curiosities as it is said to have been made without hands in the memory of the mountain pioneers and although it is at the top of a high mountain yet many of the sagacious neighbors suspect that it has no bottom. It supposedly has never been sounded with a very long line."

Nicklin further records, "Salt Pond is a sheet of fresh water ... collected during the memory of man. Formerly a rivulet ran through a hollow and escaped by sinking in the earth. It was a place frequented by cattle and their trampling stopped up the crevice so accumulations of rain and rivulets submerged the forest and formed a pond. As this was done by feet our letter writer is correct is saying it was done without hands."

The stage that ran from Red Sulphur to Salt Sulphur to Mountain Lake here seen on the Salt Sulphur Turnpike (Photo courtesy Martha Hesser)

Blacksburg Main Street as seen in the
1800's when tourists from Christiansburg
rode down it on the Salt Sulphur Turnpike
on the way to Mountain Lake
(Photo courtesy VPI & SU Special Collections)

CHAPTER 5

Antebellum Travel to Mountain Lake

In the early 1800's the Virginia springs established themselves as retreats from heat and plagues. As seen tourists from the deep south as well as the far north flocked to them in droves. Mountain Lake was not far from any of the famous spring sites. So anyone visiting the lake usually came to one of the springs first and then took the coach from one springs to another. In the circuitous route they passed Mountain Lake.

People from New Orleans and Mobile came by steamboat up the Mississippi and then up the Ohio as far as Guyandotte, Virginia, now Huntington, West Virginia. There they boarded a stage coach and came overland to White Sulphur Springs. Frederick Marryat who traveled the route from Guyandotte to White Sulphur Springs records, "In a stagecoach it is one continuation of rising ground to the springs."

People from Charleston and Savannah and the great coastal plantations of South Carolina and Georgia came up to Virginia through Asheville, North Carolina, thence to Abingdon, to Newbern and along the stage road to Pearisburg and on to the Springs.

People from Norfolk and Richmond came by stage to Christiansburg and the Montgomery County springs which were numerous - Montgomery White and Yellow, Allegheny and Crockett. From Christiansburg they took a stage to Salt, Red, Grey and White Sulphur by way of Salt Pond Mountain and passed Mountain Lake on their journey.

People from the northern cities such as Philadelphia and Baltimore came down the Valley of Virginia along the "Great Valley Road" and over the mountain to Warm Springs, thence to White Sulphur. If they wanted to travel any further they could go to Red and Salt Sulphur and over the mountains by way of Salt Pond and to the Montgomery County springs.

Many people, believe it or not, traveled this dusty, tortureous route, in a bouncing stagecoach, during the hottest days of the summer. All for the sake of their health!

In 1836 H.S. Tanner of Philadelphia, the man who published Nicklin's book, published a "New Map of Virginia with its Canals, Roads and Distances from place to place along the state and steamboat routes."

Tanner shows a road from Newbern running through Pearisburg on to Grey Sulphur Springs and then to Red Sulphur and Salt Sulphur. Salt Pond is shown though no road connects the stage road with Salt Pond. From traveler's reports we know that a road of sorts did exist.

The Virginia and Tennessee Railway was constructed to Christiansburg about 1850. This further facilitated travel to Mountain Lake. People could more quickly get to Christiansburg depot where the stage picked up travelers to the Virginia Springs and made the usual run through Blacksburg and over the mountains to Giles and up Salt Pond Mountain passing Mountain Lake. Travelers had time to view the lake before they headed over Peters Mountain to Salt Sulphur and the other springs. These early stages followed the Doe Creek road from Pembroke which was the first stagecoach or carriage route up to the lake.

Not only tourists from far away but local people were constantly at the lake. There is the poignant story of Jacob Allen Albert of the Continental Line who had been with Washington at Valley Forge. Albert was a scout and guard there for Washington and had his hands and feet frozen in that winter of despair. Discharged from Valley Forge hospital, a horse stable, he found his way home to Giles County where he lived a long life at the foot of Butt and Salt Pond Mountains.

Crippled, he always had to ride a horse or mule. One day in 1856, he was riding his mule near Mountain Lake when a storm overtook him. He got off his mule and took shelter under an overhanging cliff. The next morning his family found him, sitting upright under the cliff, the mule still waiting. Jacob had died of a heart attack at age 99.

Chapman's White Sulphur Springs
on New River later Eggleston Springs
(Photo courtesy Martha Hesser)

CHAPTER 6

Chapman's Springs and Lake Resort

Henley Chapman had assumed ownership of the Hygaen or New River White Sulphur Springs sometime before 1850. With all the tourism to the Virginia Springs Chapman saw how he could gain some profit from the old Gunpowder Springs. So he built a long rambling clapboard hotel beside New River known as Chapman's Springs and later Eggleston Springs. Chapman realized what a drawing card a side trip to his Mountain Lake would be for his New River spa.

He continued to publicize springs and lake. Having served in the Legislature in Richmond he knew how terrible the heat of that city could be in the summer. What better remedy for the fainting city dweller living in daily dread of the fevers than a rest at a cool mountain springs and lake? What better refuge for the anxious mother rushing her beautiful daughters from the dread cholera? When he mentioned the beautiful New River scenery near the Chapman Springs which by many travelers was said to compare with the Rhine Valley few could resist wanting to come to Chapman's Springs and lake.

Dr. J.J. Moorman visited the Chapman's and described them in his "Springs of Virginia" (1857) saying, "New River White Sulphur Springs is the name given a recently improved Sulphur Spring on New River in Giles County. These springs may be reached by stage either from Virginia and Tennessee Railway at Newbern or from the Red Sulphur in Monroe County."

One of the few people to record in words and pictures a trip to Chapman Springs and up to Mountain Lake at this early date was an artist from Pennsylvania. His beautiful sketches of his trip are priceless.

Lewis Miller, a folk artist from York, Pennsylvania, came to Christiansburg to visit in the 1840's and 50's. He had a brother Dr. Joseph Miller, a nephew Reverend Charles Miller, Presbyterian minister, a niece Amanda Miller Edie and her son Charles Edie. The young Charles Edie often made trips around the mountains with Miller who sketched scenes everywhere he went. In July 1853 Miller and Charles Edie along with friends decided to visit Dr. Chapman's Springs and the Salt Pond Mountain. They left Christiansburg on July 13, traveled through Blacksburg, a tiny village of houses but no university. Approaching Brush Mountain the sixteen men and women in the party were mounted on horses and riding in pairs along the road while behind followed two buggies. A Mr. Pepper and his daughter rode in one and in the other were Charles Edie and Lewis Miller. As they crossed Brush Mountain Edie got out and walked to save the horse's strength and Miller sketched Edie talking with a deer hunter. They crossed Gap Mountain and through Newport continuing on to Dr. Chapman's Springs at present Eggleston.

The Chapman's long white hotel overlooking the New River welcomed visitors. The New was very deep here - possibly 150 feet. Two weeks after this the son of the proprietor was drowned in the New. After viewing Bullard's Rocks and other scenes the guests ate at a long table where negro servants kept in motion large fans suspended from the ceiling.

Early the next morning the cavalcade started up the Doe Creek road nine miles up to the Salt Pond. Lewis Miller sketched the gay cavalcade stretched out along the road. Those on horseback outdistanced the buggies. Miller and Edie stopped at the Doe Creek mill to rest and Miller sketched the mill and cavalcade strung out on the road ahead. Miller has given us a most lovely sketch of the ascent of the Salt Pond mountain by way of the Doe Creek road. These scenes can be seen in "The Virginia Cavalcade" magazine, August, 1952.

Miller's trip to Salt Pond sent him into a reflective mood. "At once elevated and solitary upon the summit of the lofty Salt Pond Mountain our thoughts assume a more serious tone. Earthly sentiments are left below," says Miller. He was so enraptured he then wrote four lines of slightly sappy poetry. Luckily his forte was art. His beautiful sketches of the ascent of Salt Pond, of the Pond itself and the view from the north side of Salt Pond Mountain are his greatest gift to us.

From Miller's sketch of the lake we have a glimpse of what Mountain Lake resort was like on July 14, 1853. He shows not a building in sight. Only a boat on the lake reveals anything man-made in the area. Tops of trees stick out of the water showing the truth of the claim that the lake inundated part of the forest surrounding it.

Miller and Edie returned to Christiansburg and resumed their daily lives. Young Charles Edie went off to school at Hampden Sidney where another student shot him in 1857. During the Civil War few from the north visited in Christiansburg except invaders. After the war Lewis Miller returned and lived with his relatives until he died in 1888 and was buried in the Christiansburg's Craig Cemetery located under a pine grove adjacent the present livestock market.

Old Doe Creek Mill on the road to Mountain Lake (Photo courtesy Martha Hesser)

CHAPTER 7

The Mountain Lake Company

When Lewis Miller and the Christiansburg cavalcade of nearly twenty people made the long climb to Mountain Lake in 1853 they would gladly have spent the night in the beautiful surroundings of the lake but there were no accomodations. Miller in his sketches shows not a single building. The lone boat drifting on the lake was the only sign of man's ingenuity. As more people visited it did not escape the Chapmans that a hotel was needed up at the lake. Up to this point the lake had only been considered an extension of Chapman's Springs resort. Mountain Lake was viewed as a pleasant side excursion connected with Chapman's White.

If a hotel was to be built at the lake it would have to be accessible along a good road which would need maintenance. The sheer heights of Salt Pond Mountain surely made this seem a nightmare of road construction at the time. This was the heyday of the southern resorts and Henley Chapman had the faith that Mountain Lake would be lucrative enough to justify the effort. He and other prominent Giles men spearheaded the effort to organize both a road and resort company.

In March 1856 the state legislature incorporated the Mountain Lake and Salt Sulphur Springs Turnpike Company in Giles County. The Mountain Lake Company was incorporated at the same time. Edwin Booth, Joseph H. Hoge, William H. Snidow, Henley Chapman and associates composed the company.

The men who composed the company were all Giles men with the possible exception of Edwin Booth. An Edwin Booth was a popular actor in Richmond and Washington and was the father of John Wilkes Booth - whether Mountain Lake's Edwin was the same is unknown.

The turnpike was to run from Salt Sulphur Springs in Monroe by way of Mountain Lake in Giles to a point on the Virginia and Tennessee Railway in Montgomery or Pulaski. Stocks were to be sold at Yellow Sulphur by James P. Edmundson, Charles B. Gardner, John M. Thomas, John R. Philips and Harvey Black; at Newport in Giles by William H. Snidow, Charles Payne, Joseph H. Hoge, David B. Price and William B. Mason. At Giles Court House they would be sold by George D. Hoge, James D. Johnston, Guy B. French, Edward Hale and Thomas K. Ryder and at Salt Sulphur in Monroe by William Erskine, Nathaniel Harrison, Matthew Campbell, John Echols and Augustus A. Chapman. The Cumberland Gap road lying between Enoch Atkins and the town of Newport was a part of their road to be kept in proper repair but they were not allowed to charge any toll on this three mile section of road. Enoch Atkin's place was where the Mountain Lake road intersected the old county road.

The Mountain Lake Company was to have a capital of $50,000, to improve 5,000 acres and erect buildings at the lake, erect and operate saw and other mills and entertain guests. For all of this they were to be paid by the guests. Mountain Lake resort was born.

The first Mountain Lake Hotel built in 1856 seen here after the wear and tear of twenty years and a war (Photo courtesy Virginia State Library)

CHAPTER 8

The First Mountain Lake Hotel

Soon a saw mill was built and a wooden hotel made from the lumber. The first hotel building erected in 1856-57 has the same appearance and size as one of the buildings at Chapman's Springs. It was probably made from the same blueprints.

This hotel was used to accomodate stagecoach travelers from Christiansburg to Union, Monroe County, so is considered by some a stage stop rather than a hotel. However it did accomodate overnight guests so can claim to be a hotel. Hundreds of people came to the new hotel before the Civil War.

The cities of the South were nightmares to live in before and after the war. The heat made life nearly unbearable. The stench of humans and animals was fierce. Flies and mosquitoes were not only an irritant but deadly disease borne by them a constant dread. In the hot weather nearly every Southern city had an outbreak of typhoid or yellow fever. Charleston, Mobile and New Orleans had nightmarish epidemics each summer, taking hundreds of lives. Those lucky few that could afford it headed to Virginia's mountains. Mountain Lake had a special appeal because it had no mosquitoes. It was too cool at night for them to thrive.

The name of Mountain Lake resort spread through the south and north and even to Europe. It was so acclaimed that a German artist, Edward Beyer who was in Virginia from 1854 to 1857 painted the famous "Salt Pond". In his "Album of Virginia" published in 1857 he has two beautiful lithographs, one of Mountain Lake itself and one of the view from Bald Knob.
Beyer also wrote an early account of the new hotel built before the Civil War. He writes, "There is a fine carriage road (now route 613) from the New River White Sulphur Springs to the top of Salt Pond Mountain near which is a fine, large Hotel, that commends itself to the seekers of pleasure and the lovers of pure air. There are boats on the Lake for amusement, and fine hunting and trout fishing in the neighborhood. An excellent road to the Salt Sulphur will soon be completed."

Of the Salt Pond itself he says, "It is a beautiful Lake in the midst of Mountains - about one and a half-mile long and three-quarters of a mile wide. The water is perfectly transparent, and on a clear day, visitors gliding over it in a boat, can see, deep down under it, the remains of a forest."
"The water has no taste of salt, and bears the name, as the Artist was informed by Mr. Lybrook, the Hotel Proprietor at the Base of Salt Pond Mountain, from the fact that more than half a century ago, farmers used the Valley, now the bed of the Lake, to salt their cattle, which became the resorts of herds of elk, buffalo and deer. Hundreds of these wild animals have been seen around the Spring in this Valley at one time, which was gradually enlarged by their frequent visits and by their pawing up the ground around it. One morning a servant went as usual to salt his cattle, when he found the whole Valley filled with water. The rise was rapid until a gap offered at its termination to flow off

- at which point is now erected a Mill."

From this rendition we can see Edward Beyer described the origin of the lake only from local hearsay.

Concerning his artistic view of the lake, seen in this present publication, Beyer says, "The Artist has taken the view from the Salt Pond Knob, which is a half mile higher than the Lake and forms a large platform, covered with shrubbery, from which visitors have an extensive Mountain view upwards of a hundred miles in diameter, thus presenting a sublime spectacle. From this point can be seen, elevated in all their grandeur, the Peaks of Otter, the only equals in height in Virginia of the Knob. To the left is a view of the Pond, in the middle is Blacksburg and in the background are the Mountains around Christiansburg and Pilot Mountain."

Beyer not only painted the lake but he told people how to find it.

"Visitors from the South wishing to see this curiosity must leave the Cars on the Virginia and Tennessee Rail Road at Christiansburg Depot."

The Mountain Lake Turnpike Company founded in 1856 began work on the turnpike but could not complete the road due to lack of money.

The Mountain Lake Company in charge of building the hotel seems to have accomplished more. As mentioned their small hotel was running by 1857.

In the summer of 1857 or 1858 on Sunday July 18 a party from Christiansburg and Blacksburg including Amanda Palmer, Sue Palmer, William L. Kinzer and Sue E. Henderson made a trek to Newport to the home of Mrs. C. H. Payne. The party headed for the resort the next morning and Kinzer recorded their trip in his diary which is in the Virginia Historical Society.

Kinzer writes, "Went to the "Salt Pond" with the same company, increased by Mr. and Mrs. Payne and daughter. Rode and chatted with Sue Henderson. Had a poor view from the summit. Rolled balls on the Alley, rode on the lake, ate dinner, and a good one too, also rode on the pond, walked about at its mouth, rowed back, sung, laughed, played tricks, splashed water, rolled balls on the Alley two hours more, went to the Hotel, paid our bills, rode to the summit, could see nothing for the thick clouds, down the mountain we went, I with the others lodged at Wm. Surfaces."

From this we see that the new hotel was serving good meals and the new bowling alley was installed.

In January 1860 the Virginia legislature appropriated money for the Mountain Lake turnpike. Mr. John E. Alexander was Treasurer and on April 17, 1860 he reported that the legislature had money available for building the turnpike. He wrote asking what the company must do to draw on the fund. He reports that the company at that time had a number of hands at work on the road attempting to complete it for summer travel.

Mr. Alexander also wrote the Board of Public Works that a meeting would be held at Mountain Lake to carry out the instructions of the Board.

On May 3, 1860 the meeting of the stockholders of the

Mountain Lake and Salt Sulphur Turnpike Company was held at Mountain Lake. William H. Snidow was called to chair the meeting with John E. Alexander as Secretary. Edwin G. Amiss and Alexander were recommended as directors. Joseph H. Hoge as proxy for the Montgomery White Sulphur Springs Company became a subscriber to the Company for 128 shares of stock.

The route of the Mountain Lake-Salt Sulphur Springs Turnpike was finalized. It would run from Goodwin's Ferry to Kire (near the present West Virginia line which did not exist at that time). From Kire it would run across Peter's Mountain along the route following the Stony Creek road. Here it connected with an early stage road which ran from near Union in Monroe County through Salt Sulphur Springs over Peter's Mountain and White Oak Mountain to Stony Creek, thence to Mountain Lake.

By 1860 Henley Chapman had become old and had turned Chapman's Springs over to William Eggleston. On July 3, 1860 the Richmond "Daily Dispatch" ran the following ad:

"The New River White Sulphur Springs are situated immediately on the banks of this beautiful stream in Giles county, Virginia, about twenty-two miles from the Montgomery White and the Yellow Sulphur Springs, and about eight miles from the celebrated Salt Pond or Mountain Lake."

"There will be a comfortable daily Stage from Montgomery White and Yellow, and a tri-weekly from New River Springs, connecting at Giles Court House with the line to the Red, Salt and White Sulphur Springs."

"Parties wishing to visit Salt Pond or Mountain Lake will find constant conveyance thereto."

"Post Office address: Eggleston Springs, Giles county, Virginia.'"

"Wm. Eggleston, Prop'r."

From this period on the New River White Sulphur or Chapman Springs were called "Eggleston Springs". As seen they were advertized widely and Mountain Lake was considered a side trip connected to Eggleston Springs.

In 1861 a fourteen-year-old boy William G. Pendleton came to visit his uncle Albert C. Pendleton at Pearisburg. He recalls, "During the visit I went to the "Salt Pond" as it was then called, with a party of young people" among whom were Henley Chapman's grandchildren.

"With the Chapman boys I rowed out on the lake," says Pendleton. We could see large forest trees still standing erect in the lake beneath the crystal water. After returning I made a visit to Mt. Pleasant the home of Mr. Chapman near the mouth of Walker's Creek. The old gentleman was fond of playing checkers. While we were playing checkers I mentioned my visit to the "Salt Pond." He said the trees I had seen in the lake were there, alive and full of foliage in the summer time, when he salted his cattle in the basin and before the water began to accumulate in a body."

Because of this conversation with Henley Chapman young Pendleton received a false impression that there had never been a permanent lake at Mountain Lake and he states this as a fact in his "History of Tazewell County, Virginia". However studies of twentieth century scientists show that a body of water continually changing size due to weather changes has existed on Salt Pond Mountain for over 9,000 years.

Beyer's view of Mountain Lake about 1856 (Photo courtesy VPI & SU Special Collections)

CHAPTER 9

War

Young William Pendleton's visit to Mountain Lake the summer of 1861 was overshadowed by the war that had just begun. Virginia had seceded taking Giles County with her so Mountain Lake was in the new Confederate States of America. The western counties of Virginia seceded from Virginia and stayed in the Union. Monroe County just across the county line from Mountain Lake was in the new state of West Virginia, the newest state in the United States. Therefore Salt Sulphur Springs just over Peters Mountain from Salt Pond was still in the Union. William Erskine, owner of Salt Sulphur Springs, was a suspected Union man because he would not let Rebels stay in his resort houses.

Mountain Lake could still be visited by Confederate guests but the old Salt Pond-Salt Sulphur stage by 1863 had stopped carrying passengers from Mountain Lake to Salt Sulphur. Any traveler now riding it would find himself in Union territory. Not that Union sympathy was lacking around Mountain Lake. In fact it appears from future events that among the native people there were many Unionists.

The Ballard family at Ballard in Monroe were Unionists. William Ballard and his large family as well as Dr. Ballard who kept a store on the road from Giles to Monroe were Unionists. Because of Dr. Ballard's sympathies his store was robbed by troops of Confederate General Floyd. Porterfield girls from nearby Salt Pond Mountain had married Ballards and some of their brothers believed in the Union.

Some of the Lafon and Martin families who lived on Salt Pond near Mountain Lake were still loyal. There were other mountain families who still believed in the Constitution of the United States no matter what the government in Richmond decreed.

By fall of 1861 the Union Army under the command of Colonel Rutherford B. Hayes, later President of the United States, had a camp at Raleigh, present Beckley, West Virginia. Here they were gathering information about the rebel territory to the east in the Virginia mountains. A Methodist Episcopal minister, Russell G. French of Mercer County, had been driven from his home because he was a Union man. French became a guide and informant for Hayes. Also an escaped Negro slave named Charles Clark whose wife had been sold south became an informant for Hayes. This former slave gives excellent verbal pictures of conditions in the Monroe-Giles area which included Salt Pond Mountain and Mountain Lake.

The ex-slave Clark said that Confederate rich men's sons were getting discharges from the army. Poor men's sons did not. Patrols were out to keep slaves of rich men at home but the Confederates were "pressing" poor folks to man the patrols. There was much grumbling over poor folks being compelled to patrol to keep rich men's slaves from running off. There was grumbling about poor folks' horses being taken for the Confederate Army while rich men's horses were not taken.

Two men who had been instrumental in building the Salt

Sulphur-Salt Pond Turnpike to Mountain Lake were now prominent Confederate leaders. General Augustus Chapman was the leading military figure in Monroe and John Echols who according to the ex-slave Clark, "lived in a fine mansion at Union" in Monroe was now a Confederate Colonel. These men had bought and incorporated Old Sweet Springs in 1852 and had naturally pushed the completion of the Salt Sulphur-Salt Pond Turnpike which would bring tourists first to Mountain Lake and then on to their springs. Soon they would desperately have to use the road they had promoted to Mountain Lake.

For strategic reasons the Union Army wanted to destroyed the Virginia and Tennessee Railroad at Newbern and the bridge across New River (at present Radford) over which visitors had once traveled to Mountain Lake. Hoping to rush in and destroy this railroad Hayes asked Clark about distances to it.

Hoping to get to Newbern Hayes' soldiers came into Pearisburg on May 6, 1862. Hayes described the country along New River as "romantic, highly cultivated and beautiful." "Giles Court House is a neat pretty village with a most magnificent surrounding country both as regards scenery and cultivation."

"These people have all been Secesh but are polite and intelligent. When Major Comly, Captain Gilmore and Captain Drake entered town the people were standing on the corners idly gossiping."

The Union force established a camp, put out guards and settled in to stay in Pearisburg. Hayes said, "I find more intelligence and culture here than anywhere else in Virginia. This is a lovely spot, fine clean village, most beautiful and romantic surrounding country and a polite and educated people."

"The taking of Giles Court House is one of the boldest things of the War. It was perfectly impudent. There were more Secesh standing on the corners than there were in the party with Major Comly when they dashed in."

Hayes' final tribute was, "The beautiful cultivated country along the banks of New River has ruined me for living in the tame level country of Ohio."

Hayes' plan to use Pearisburg as a base from which to launch a Union Army attack on the railroad came to nought. Confederate General Heth chased them out and all the way back to Lewisburg where Heth himself was stopped cold by another Union force. Colonel George Crook and his 36th Ohio pounced upon Heth and defeated him. Soon Colonel Crook became General Crook. This man would play a vivid role in the history of Mountain Lake.

CHAPTER 10

Droop Mountain Defeat

Late in 1863 the Union Army organized another push to invade Virginia and destroy the Virginia and Tennessee railroad at Dublin and the New River Bridge. General W.W. Averell would lead this raid to Lewisburg and dash on through to Newbern. Probably he planned to use the new turnpike road across Salt Pond Mountain to get to New River. On November 6, 1863 moving over the mountains from Beverly heading to Lewisburg Averell encountered Confederates blocking the road at Droop Mountain near present Hillsboro in Pocahontas County. Colonel John Echols's troops faced Averell. Echols would accompany Jefferson Davis south when the Confederacy fell.

Now at Droop Mountain he had blocked the Union advance with felled timber across the roads. His 4,000 men and 7 cannon were dug in so Averell made a lengthy detour of nine miles to the rear of Echols attacking and defeating him. Hotly pressed by Major Gibson's Cavalry until night Echols was forced to retreat or scatter into the woods heading toward Union. Colonel George S. Patton's Brigade and one regiment of Jenkins were slashed and cut up by the Federals. It was a defeat that would have galled General George S. Patton descendant of the Colonel. Averell says "The enemy retreat a total rout, the victory was decisive. His forces threw away their arms, scattered in every direction."

Averell headed on to Lewisburg joining Duffie arriving November 7 to clear out remnants of Rebel opposition. He had orders to continue on to destroy the railroad on New River but his losses were heavy, his men footsore and starving so he could not.

Meanwhile the Confederates retreated along the Salt Sulphur-Salt Pond Turnpike. The Confederate War Department in Richmond telegraphed General Lee in Culpepper, "General Echols has been defeated with heavy loss and is endeavoring to retreat by Salt Pond Mountain. Enemy advancing about 7,000 strong. Can you send aid?"

General Sam Jones commander of the department of western Virginia rushed to the Confederate Depot at Dublin and telegraphed, "Echols' men will retreat by Salt Pond Mountain if he can but I fear he cannot escape and will be cut up and destroyed."

Col. J.M. Wade in Christiansburg was ordered, "Take your entire force to Salt Pond Mountain to meet General Echols."

This same day Colonel William Wiley Arnett had gotten some of Echol's men near Salt Pond Mountain and from there sent a dispatch telling of his part at Droop Mountain. Echols with another remnant got to Salt Pond Mountain on the night of November 8 and there camped.

By November 10 Jones had gone from Narrows up to Salt Pond Mountain and reported, "General Echol's brigade has not I think had as many in killed and wounded as I first supposed. One battalion was engaged and is approaching this place by way of Sweet Springs and ought to be in today. I think Echols will have them in fighting condition in a few days."

General Jones also reports, "I met Brigadier General Echols' command on Salt Pond Mountain. It was promptly supplied with the necessary arms and clothing and in four days moved back and reoccupied points it had occupied before the engagement on November 6." Also the Confederates claimed that the "affair at Droop Mountain was by no means as disastrous as at first reported."

Although not mentioned in official reports, local people say some of Echols'men from this defeat at Droop Mountain followed the Salt Pond road pass Mountain Lake and down the mountain nearly to Newport disbanding at the site of the Red Covered Bridge at the foot of present Mountain Lake road.

Averell and Duffie meanwhile were at Lewisburg licking their wounds. General Jones said, "The enemy was so severely punished as to deter him from following up the advantage. After a long and fruitless march he suffered heavier loss than he inflicted."

Because of these losses and bad December weather Averell had to postpone the raid on New River Bridge. But it was not forgotten. They would try again in the spring.

General W.W. Averell led his cavalry over Salt Pond Mountain in their flight from pursuing Confederates (Photo courtesy Library of Congress)

CHAPTER 11

Crook's Campaign and Mountain Lake

In January 1864 General George Crook took command of the 2d Division of the United States Army, known as the "Kanawha Division". Headquarters was at Charleston, West Virginia, and he was given orders to march from there into Virginia and destroy the Virginia and Tennessee Railroad, the Confederate supply depot at Dublin and the New River Railroad Bridge. He was then to join other Federal forces and advance toward Lynchburg where they would set up a Federal operations center.

Crook's Army reached Cloyd's Mountain in Pulaski County and fought one of the bloodiest battles of the entire Civil War on May 9. He destroyed the Dublin Depot and New River Railroad Bridge. At Dublin he got news of Confederate forces advancing upon him. By now he was far from his supply base with many wounded and prisoners as well as 6,000 men to feed. He knew he could not stand a Confederate attack so changed his plans and rapidly moved toward West Virginia. He crossed the New River at Pepper's Ferry (present Route 114 bridge) and moved into Blacksburg. From there he marched his men westward on the Salt Pond-Salt Sulphur road that the tourists had gaily traveled before the war. Now there was little gaiety. Ambulances full of wounded clogged the road. Over two hundred slaves who had left their masters followed along after the army - some on foot and some in makeshift vehicles jamming the road. A long line of Confederate prisoners hungry and barefoot followed along. The mass of Union soldiers had little food so were on the point of starvation. To complicate matters torrential rains had been pouring for two days with no sign of stopping. Under these great difficulties the Kanawha Division of the United States Army marched out of Blacksburg toward Newport in Giles County.
Waiting at Newport was a small Confederate force and Crook had to shell the town about an hour as well as advance his skirmishers in every direction around the town to break through the village. After a short delay, the army marched on.

General George Crook who led the "Kanawha Division" past Mountain Lake on its escape into West Virginia (Photo courtesy National Archives)

Fight at the Junction of Salt Pond Road

Colonel Frost's 11th West Virginians, placed in front of Crook's army, fought their way through Newport and on the road over Payne's hill down the Pearisburg-Narrows road, present Route 460. They were pushing toward the junction of the Mountain Lake-Salt Sulphur Turnpike road so they could clear that for the army to march through. But just over Payne's Hill they ran into their old foe Colonel William Lowther Jackson's 19th West Virginia Cavalry who rushing from West Virginia had established themselves near the junction. Jackson was commonly called "Mudwall" to distinguish him from his more famous cousin "Stonewall" Jackson. Before the war "Mudwall" had actually been a more important man in Virginia than "Stonewall". Born in Clarksburg, he had served in the House of Delegates, as Virginia's State Auditor and Lieutenant Governor. When the war began he enlisted as a private, became an aid to cousin "Stonewall" and was rapidly promoted. He had fought Averell at Huttonsville, West Virginia, and on the "Big Salem Raid". In spring of '64 his command had been stationed at Warm Springs to prevent Federal invasion from West Virginia such as was now occurring. He had rushed his force toward Crook but had gotten only as far as the Salt Pond road when Crook pushed through Newport.

As Crook's men advanced out of Newport they were in battle formation. Captain David Poe, one of "Mudwall's" men watching them advance says, "I was sent with a heavy skirmish line to meet Crook. He was coming down a draft. I was on one side of the road and another officer on the other side. General Crook did not send out a skirmish line to meet us but brought up a line of battle."

Here at the Salt Pond junction where the present Mountain Lake road intersects Route 460, the 11th West Virginia tore into Jackson's force in fierce skirmishing. The 11th West Virginians hated Jackson's 19th for in it were partisan bands like the Mocassin Rangers. Many men in the 11th had been driven from their homes in counties of West Virginia overrun by partisans. Co. A in the 19th was the Mocassin Rangers under Captain George Downs, one of the most dangerous partisan bands in West Virginia. William Harman's band which Crook's army had fought after crossing East River Mountain was another. The 11th had fought Downs and Harman all over West Virginia.

"Mudwall", commanding partisans, had asked the 11th to surrender to him at the battle of Bulltown to which they replied, "We will fight till hell freezes over and if we have to retreat we will retreat on ice."

Jackson reports "considerable skirmishing" here at the junction with the 11th. This time the scales were tipped in favor of the 11th. They did not have to face him alone. Crook's army of thousands was moving rapidly in battle formation behind them. Jackson reports, "Crook tried to surround us on all sides."

Frost and his West Virginians fought valiantly and cleared the junction. In the same kind of action later in the summer Frost would die at Snicker's Gap but here he lived to clear the entrance to the Salt Pond road so the army could begin the climb to Mountain Lake.

Confederate Captain David Poe says, "As we had but a small force, General Jackson pulled his men off to one side and let General Crook pass on westward with a little skirmishing crossing over Pond Mountain."

Of this action future president Rutherford Hayes says, "Met "Mudwall" Jackson and fifteen hundred men - a poor force that lit out rapidly from near Newport."

Hayes calls it a "poor force" and "Mudwall's" Captain Poe agrees saying, "Most of our brigade was dismounted and were on a forced march. Our old shoes and boots were fast giving out. Many were barefooted long before we met the enemy." As they hurried toward Newport, Poe says, "I, myself, had marched two or three days in my bare feet in snow and rain."

E.C. Arthur in the 23rd Ohio band reports of the junction fight, "The Johnnies were driven without serious harm, unless it was to the terror stricken negroes, who would pile down off their loaded vehicles when all on foot would fly for the trees at the report of a rifle."

Mudwall's men left a mess of equipment in the road. A 91st Ohio trooper says, "They left considerable booty in our possession."

One of Crook's Pennsylvanians reports, "They left in such a hurry they forgot to take their baggage with them." Knapsacks, blankets, camp and garrison equipment, commissary stores were all lying about. Colonel Morris says, "They left behind 2 wagons loaded with supplies and one dead man, who was killed by our skirmishers."

About this man, musician Andy Stairwalt reports, "We captured a rebble officer who was mortal wounded. He was a bold man, had pluck to the last. He showed fight to the last. His little force left him going in the direction of Giles Court House."

Crook ordered all of "Mudwall's" deserted equipment destroyed by Sickel's Pennsylvanians, a fitting assignment considering the practice they had in property destruction around Blacksburg.

Here at the junction fight with Jackson, General Crook and his staff took a "breather". They rested at the Charles Atkins home which had nearly been hit by Federal shells. Today an old frame house where Charles Atkins lived in the 1930's still stands on the Atkins property at the junction of Mountain Lake road with the present Route 460. The author visited Atkins many times in the late 1930's and heard him tell her father how General Crook and his army had stopped there and many details of their march through Giles County.

Crook ordered all the Atkin's horses seized to pull his cannon and ambulances and all the meat taken for his hungry men.

While his men were searching for the meat and rounding up the horses the Atkins family pleaded with him to spare their horses. "After much pleading he ordered his men to release all the Atkins horses which they had rounded up. However they carried away considerable meat," so reported Charles Atkins, a teenager at the time.

Meanwhile Colonel Frost, 11th West Virginia, reports, "My battalion was placed on the road about half a mile from the intersection with Salt Pond road to prevent attack upon our train."

This force was definitely needed. Though Jackson had fled Colonel French would send back 350 men under Colonel Joseph W. Kesler of Jackson's command to harass Crook "in every conceivable manner."

Soldier E.C. Arthur reports, "After leaving Newport we waded a creek and began the ascent of Salt Pond Mountain."

This creek is Sinking Creek. In the early 1900's a red covered bridge was built over the creek where the Union army had waded across. Today that has been replaced by a modern bridge near the Mountain Lake resort sign.

Crook sent some Ohioans from McMullin's Battery under Lieutenant Fee up Salt Pond road with three cannon. Fee placed these cannon on the south slope of Salt Pond Mountain where they had a good command of the valley below and could shell Jackson should he return.

Jackson's men went on the Pearisburg road to the residence of Captain J. H. Hoge at the base of Salt Pond Mountain where they established camp for the night. Here they remained as Crook's army passed up the Salt Pond road.

Adjutant Hastings who did not drink Mountain Lake water (Photo courtesy U.S. Army Military History Institute)

Lieutenant William McKinley, later President, as he looked in the Union Army at Mountain Lake (Photo courtesy West Virginia Dept. of Culture and History)

CHAPTER 12

Ascent of Salt Pond Mountain

When the army cleared Salt Pond junction they began the slow climb up the mountain. Three guns had been sent ahead with Lieutenant Fee's men to cover them, then the infantry marched through followed by the wagon train. The officer in charge of the train was Rutherford Hayes who records in his journal for Thursday, May 12, "A most disagreeable rainy day. My brigade had charge of the train. I acted as wagonmaster; a long train to keep up. Rode all day in mud and rain back and forth."

"There are few in General Crook's army at least in the First Brigade who will ever forget that long and dreary march through the darkness, rain and mud up this mountain," remembers one Union boy.

" The wagons occupied the main road, which left but little room for us to pick our way along its edge, frequently elbowing our way through groups of contrabands who were huddled together by the road side, and not without some danger of slipping off the narrow path and plunging into the ravines below."

E. C. Arthur remembers "the melancholy bray of the poor tired mules as they cried out against their masters, who were plying the merciless blacksnake whips into their steaming flanks."

Colonel Frost's men remained in their position as guards until all the wagons had passed the junction, then they followed as rear guard to the camp at the top of Salt Pond.

"Mudwall" Jackson's men had gone into night camp at Hoge's plantation today owned by Dr. Moore. They were not strong enough to stop Crook. David Poe one of Jackson's men describes the scene. He says they closely watched Crook's advance up the Salt Pond road but did not attempt to interfere. Union soldier E.C. Arthur agrees that both forces "were in close proximity and only a cloud hanging over the ravines separated them which had it lifted would have exposed both columns to view. General Jackson's forces remained perfectly quiet and permitted the Union army also the train which came along later and at night to pass unmolested."

The scene as the army slowly climbed along Salt Pond road was certainly nothing like the gay cavalcade that had accompanied Lewis Miller in 1853. It was a desperate hungry horde that now toiled upward. As he climbed along the mountain road Captain Michael Egan remembers the hunger. "Whoever participated in this raid, can never forget the biting pangs of hunger. In strict observance of the orders of the general prohibiting foraging or straggling, I suffered keenly from want of something to eat". He says a Captain S. Porter, Company K, 15th West Virginia, gave him some food. Though there were some rations issued the men, none were issued the officers.

Charles Atkins related that the Union troops were dragging along a brass cannon which they had placed on Newport hill and in firing toward the retreating Confederates had nearly hit his house. As mentioned it is doubtful it was the brass Napoleon captured at Cloyd's Mountain. Hayes says they did bring two cannon up and over the mountain through the mud and got them to West Virginia. Major Comly of Hayes' staff says, "The two pieces of artillery captured by the 23rd at Cloyd's Mountain were brought off with incredible pains by a detail from the regiment under Lieutenant Austin."

According to tradition the army camped briefly several miles up Mountain Lake road from the junction in level fields where today stands a red-roofed Victorian house. It was at this point that General Crook ordered no straggling or foraging in the area. However it is known that Ben Porterfield's place was combed for chickens, hams, meal or anything else edible. It was also here that the general ordered the soldiers to gather together all their loot robbed from houses along the march and turn all over to their officers. Due to this order the soldiers pooled their loot and hid it under rocks on this farm. Attempts have been made in vain to find this cache.

About a mile beyond this Victorian house, McMullin's First Ohio Battery's three cannons on the south slope of Salt Pond mountain fired ten rounds towards "a force under Jackson." Today travelers pass a large log house sitting in a sharp curve of the Mountain Lake road. Up the mountain at the next curve is the site where the Ohio battery placed their cannons to fire toward Jackson's troops in the vicinity of the junction.

As the army climbed further up the mountain they came to a curve near Virginia Tech's present Horton Center. On Smith's curve just below Horton Center or at the Sam Bailey place just above the army posted a cannon which fired on the Hoge place. Due to mist and fog the cannoneers did not score a hit but cannon balls were later found in the grounds behind the Hoge mansion. This was a gesture of defiance because "Mudwall" Jackson's troops had gone into camp there for the night.

Present-day Mountain Lake gossip says that the Porterfields, a large clan living on the mountain, urged Union officers to shell the Hoge mansion because of a grudge. Many of the Porterfields were Confederate sympathesizers and would not have done this. The author is a descendant of the Unionists in the family. An uncle, Lewis Flavius Porterfield, known as "Lute" was serving as a guide for General Crook. No one has ever claimed "Lute" had anything to do with the soldiers firing on the Hoge's place.

The only light the present author can shed on this present gossip is that her grandfather Jay Burk Porterfield's mother Mary Burk Williams, daughter of George Williams who owned the Hoge estate grew to womanhood on this property. In the 1840's her brothers sold to the Hoges and went west to Livingston County, Missouri, with the Giles County Caravan. Mary and husband, George A. Porterfield, brother of Lute and father of Jay, went to Missouri. Finding it inhospitable they returned to Virginia. The author's family have a walnut highboy that went from Virginia to Missouri and back in a covered wagon. About 1842 the Hoge's built the present Hoge mansion, "Wheatlands" and were well established on the property Mary Williams Porterfield's brothers had sold to the Hoges. Since her father's land and her childhood home had been sold to the Hoges, Mary Porterfield could not go back to her childhood home but lived in Newport where her husband established a small Latin school beside the road that Crook's army would march along. There may have been bitterness about the loss of the Williams estate with Mary and transmitted to Lute and Jay. Whether they were so infected as to ask Union soldiers to fire on the Hoge's home is unknown and unlikely. It is doubtful officers would have allowed soldiers to fire cannon on a flimsy whim of some local person.

The real reason they fired on the Hoge place was to defy Jackson's men who had gone into camp there temporarily.

Mountain Lake gossip also has that Union soldiers pushed a cannon over the mountainside either somewhere along the road or after they got to the top of the mountain. Marshall Huffman of Clover Hollow near Newport told the author's father that once when hunting he had seen a cannon down in a ravine in a place impossible to retrieve. Crook's men had seen a mule fall off East River mountain and become trapped among the rocks. This may have given someone the bright idea of pushing a cannon into such a position. Nothing has been found in official records to support a story of a deserted cannon pushed over the mountainside on Salt Pond Mountain. Colonel Sickel reports a gun carriage of a captured cannon lost when a driver carelessly allowed it to run over a precipice beyond the Greenbrier River on the Blue Sulphur road. This occurred in West Virginia and possibly is the origin of the story of a cannon pushed over a mountainside.

However Crook does say that the road was nearly impassable, the wagons up to their beds in mud. Some wagons were deserted before the army got to Mountain Lake. In ravines above the Horton Center piles of wagon wheels and other items were found as late as the 1940's. The artillery chief said he lost seventeen horses. Without horses to pull carriages and guns it is possible a cannon received a push and waits to be found. Further up the mountain the next day cannon are also said to have been abandoned.
Major Comly reports, "The animals were much fagged by heavy work and insufficient rest. Many dropped dead in the harness. Loads had to be shifted, a number of wagons abandoned and burned."

The men and wagon train stretched all the way up the mountainside during the evening and night of May 12. "Much of our train could not get into camp this night," reported Crook, "but was strung out over Salt Pond Mountain."

A camp had been established all along the right and left banks of Mountain Lake and on up to Hogskin Creek.

The train was a long affair. There were now about 10,000 people struggling up the mountain including the army, prisoners and slaves. There were thousands of horses and mules, possibly 50 or 60 wagons loaded with two hundred wounded men.

Rutherford Hayes says, "One of the most interesting and affecting things is the train of contrabands, old and young, male and female, one hundred to two hundred - toiling uncomplainingly along with the army."

Of these slaves Major Comly says, "To add to the confusion a large number of contrabands who had joined the column with all sorts of conveyances and many with none began to lose horses and wagons which clogged the road and many of the poor wretches had to walk through mud and rain carrying children and supplies and whatever household goods they were unwilling to leave."

A camp was established on the right and left banks of Mountain Lake. Colonel Morris says his men got into camp about sundown. Michael Egan says, "Just as night was falling, we halted on the borders of a small salt lake, a remarkable body of water. When the teams came up, I inspected a wagon and found a box of hardtack snugly stowed away in a corner by a driver. He whined piteously when I confiscated his "few crackers". I divided the contents of the box impartially among my company all of whom were well-nigh famished."

Hayes' 23rd Ohio reports, "We got to camp at midnight." Though rain poured, one soldier comments, "There were no tents."

"It was late at night when we arrived at the top of the mountain", says E.C. Arthur, 23rd Ohio band, "having marched sixteen miles, eight of them up this mountain. With neither supper or shelter we curled ourselves down on the wet leaves in the woods, like spokes to a wagon wheel around a big fire and forgetting all the trials of the day were soon asleep in the rain, unconscious of our neighbors, the enemy, just over the ravine."

Hayes the future President of the United States says, "I slept on wet ground without blankets. A horrible day, one of the worst of all my experience. Fifteen miles traveled." Later at a Union veteran's reunion Hayes as guest speaker spoke particularly of the horrendous crossing of Crook's army over Salt Pond Mountain.

Meanwhile Frost's West Virginians were guarding the junction at the foot of the mountain. When all the train had cleared they followed as rear guard to the camp. Frost says, "We reached the camp on Salt Pond Mountain in the midst of a heavy rain, without shelter or food."

Though heavy rain had prevailed most of the day making their advance very slow and there had been constant skirmishing and straggling at Blacksburg, Newport and beyond, the Union army reported no casualties in its ascent of Salt Pond Mountain or at the lake.

This night of May 12 while Crook's army was strung out on Salt Pond Mountain, his cavalry under General W.W. Averell had arrived in Christiansburg hoping to follow Crook over Salt Pond Mountain the next day.

CHAPTER 13

Salt Pond Mountain

On the morning of May 13 General Crook awoke in his water-logged encampment on the top of Salt Pond Mountain. His troops had slept in their encampment by Mountain Lake only a few hours when they were aroused about 4:30 in the morning.

" We were awakened by buglers before 5 o'clock," remembers E.C. Arthur, "to find the same cold, clammy and sticky rain had not abated and ourselves chilled, sore and stiff, after our march from Blacksburg."

It had rained all night. Crook's miserable men were strung out all the way up the mountain road and in the encampment at the mountain top to the right and left of the lake. Some of the troops were already moving out when Major Comly's rear guard reached camp at 5:30 in the morning after what Comly says was "the most laborious and miserable 24 hours work the Regiment had ever gone through."

At this time Mountain Lake, which today is a world famous resort, was a small but well known southern resort. It had a small wooden framed hotel, a bowling alley beside the lake and a few rickety boats. Many still thought it was a salt lake. Several officers in this expedition call it Salt Lake in their dispatches and journals. The whole place seemed entirely deserted when the army camped at the lake. The hotel ordinarily did not open until June 1 and anyway noone was going to be around to welcome a Yankee army.

"With nothing to eat since leaving Pepper's Ferry but a light supper on the evening of the 11th, when we enjoyed some very fine Virginia ham and potatoes boiled with their jackets on," says E.C. Arthur, "we were in a condition to appreciate a first class hotel, summer resort, or even a second class restaurant."

"With nothing to cook or eat in sight some of us whiled away the breakfast hour with a ramble in the rain, about this famous summer resort. We found the hotel, where we would gladly have registered for breakfast, but it was too early in the morning and the season to be open. A bowling alley and the little lake was about all there was to admire. A short distance was the hotel where we would gladly have registered for breakfast."

"Of all the summer resorts in both Virginias, none is more attractive or interesting than "Salt Pond Mountain" or Mountain Lake as it is now called," writes E.C. Arthur in the 1880's. "The name changed to correct the erroneous idea that the lake is a body of salt water as some have described. To the contrary Mountain Lake is a sheet of pure transparent spring water covering 50 acres, one hundred feet in depth. The existence of a lake at so great an elevation above tide, and so near the summit of a high mountain is almost without precedent."

Everyone in Crook's army was not as informed as Arthur. Adjutant Hastings said, "This body of water is as salt as any sea, a strange condition which none can account for."

To make such a statement we assume this adjutant went up the

Salt Pond road with his head literally in the clouds. Certainly he never bothered to actually taste the water himself.

Other soldiers drank from the lake and one said, "At this beautiful lake we filled our canteens, arranged our toilets and returned to our friendly campfire which was to the right of the road at the mountain top. Whatever may be said of this popular resort, it certainly offered very poor accomodations to General Crook and his tired soldiers and it is probable never before or since entertained the same number of uninvited guests on so short a notice or fare. We will not judge them inhospitable for had they known we were coming that way, we would undoubtedly have received a warmer reception."

Back at their camp these men found Colonel Rutherford Hayes "in quiet mediation seated on a stump in the woods near the fire at which he and his staff had slept the night before without shelter in the rain. The cold rain was running off his slouch hat onto his rubber blanket which he wore about his shoulders. One of his soldiers stepped up to him and apologizing, offered him a little coffee in an old dinged tin cup, that had been blackened over many a camp fire. Another, after a diligent search, handed him a few pieces of scales of crackers that after rolling about in haversacks were delicately fringed with grease, all of which he accepted with thanks, dispatched with relish, after which he engaged in a short conversation complimentary to General Crook and his successful expedition."

This handful of cracker crumbs was the breakfast a future president of the United States enjoyed on his visit to Mountain Lake resort. Lieutenant William McKinley staff member of Hayes and another future president being only a Lieutenant did not even get crumbs. We wonder if these two future presidents ever talked of their trek through the mountains of Virginia, the vicious passage across Salt Pond Mountain and their visit to Mountain Lake resort. Hayes wrote his wife that he wanted to bring her to visit the Virginia resorts after the war but we do not know if they ever got to Mountain Lake.

General Crook had Third Brigade under Colonel Sickel march out first. Sickel in turn sent Frost's 11th West Virginia to cross Peter's Mountain first and take a position on the other side to prevent the enemy from ambushing the army as it marched along. Frost said this expedition was the 11th's first active field service and they showed commendable patience with no rations and many of them barefooted.

Possibly the guide Lute Porterfield and Frank Ballard, later commissioned by Governor Boreman, captain of a West Virginia independent company of rangers who ranged in the Monroe County mountains near Mountain Lake, was with the 11th. These rangers were active in 1864-65 helping to maintain the Union presence in these mountaineous areas as the Confederacy fell.

The work of Ballard's rangers was in the future months. Now as Crook's army marched out passing Mountain Lake one of them says, "For some distance we were commenting on the unusually dark morning when we were made aware that we were actually marching above the clouds at 4,400 feet above sea level. Below us in the valleys and ravines the clouds like huge masses of dark draperies could be seen. Above us and at the side long veils of smoke were trailing. Among some irreverent remarks that passed that morning was the warning that unless some of us changed our ways we were nearer heaven or higher up in the world than we would ever be again."

"Leaving Salt Pond mountain we marched along its summit passing Mountain Lake to our right when we began descending the mountain, near the base of which we waded Little Stony Creek. Here we halted for a time until the long train had stretched itself along the road in motion to catch up with the column when we resumed our march up the winding road and over Pott's Mountain."

Apparently it was during this halt that Crook ordered the destruction of equipment. He says, "The wagons in many places would go down to their beds in the mud. Many of the teams were giving out, and we had no forage for them, and had Peter's Mountain yet to cross before we could get any. I was compelled to destroy some of my loads so as to lighten up my wagons. A great deal of this transportation was received just on the eve of our departure from Charleston when it was too late to get any other, it being sent to the rear from our large armies as being unserviceable".

Albert Wright, 3rd Pennsylvania, says, "We had to throw most of the baggage away. I lost a knapsack."

West Virginia trooper Reader says, "We burned about 40 wagons and 700 guns which we had captured." He mentions not mud but "a regiment following our rear guard" which we know were "Mudwall" Jackson's men as the reason for this destruction. For by this time "Mudwall" had his men marching up Salt Pond Mountain either following along the turnpike or coming up the Doe Creek road. He kept a safe distance from Crook but knew he could lay in wait for Averell's cavalry who would soon be coming along.
There has been great debate about exactly what Crook deserted here on Salt Pond Mountain. It seems quite positive that he must have deserted cannon. One artillery chief reported later that he lost 17 horses on this mountain so without horses to pull cannon and caissons there must have been deserted cannon.

Also with the army were their captured cannon. Rutherford Hayes claims his 23rd Ohio captured two of them. Crook had brought nearly a dozen cannon from Charleston which they were still dragging along. Although Crook claims to have gotten back to Meadow Bluff with his train intact local residents around Salt Pond mountain say cannon were junked during this destruction of equipment. One eighty-five year old resident of Newport says he remembers hearing the local men who were living in May 1864 say that the Union soldiers dug into the roadbed and buried cannon in the middle of the road, covered them up and ran wagons and horses over the spot. Cannonballs were found all over the mountain for years, one of them for many years displayed in Miller Brothers Store in Newport.

The site of this destruction stretches from Hogskin Branch behind Mountain Lake on beyond the University of Virginia Biological Station and on up Minie Ball Hill. The dumping and destruction took place for some distance along the road in this vicinity.

The present Minie Ball Hill sign beside the road is not where Minie Ball Hill actually is located. The sign is for tourist convenience while the actual site is some distance from the road.

This equipment was abandoned after being made useless and material that could be burned was set on fire.

Then the army moved out again.

At 3:00 p.m. the 23rd Ohio was ordered to cross Peter's Mountain to get forage and their Colonel Hayes says they marched fifteen miles and bivouacked at the foot of Peter's Mountain on the northeast side.

Meanwhile General Averell's cavalry had been repulsed at Gap Mountain and could not pass through Newport as Crook had done. So they had to take a circuitous route through the mountains into Craig County to John's Creek. They followed War Branch Trail along War Spur a tributary of John's Creek to its head on Salt Pond Mountain. This trail comes out today where the National Park hiking trail is on the road behind Mountain Lake near the Biological Station. This put Averell's troops on the Salt Pond-Salt Sulphur Turnpike which Crook was marching along - only Averell was a day's travel behind Crook.

Friday the 13th has always been considered unlucky. This day was no exception. Crook had to destroy his own equipment and Averell was not lucky enough to break through the pass at Gap Mountain and had to make a desperate flight through the mountains. Neither McCausland nor Jackson had trapped Averell as they had wanted. Morgan's men overran the Cloyd's Farm battlefield hospital causing unnecessary suffering for the wounded soldiers. Union doctors had their surgical instruments seized in the middle of amputations and Confederate General Jenkins had his arm amputated. These negative events we know about. We do not know how many young men, Union and Confederate, died this day at the farm hospital or were drowned in some mountain stream or downed by a bushwhacker's bullet on the road beyond Mountain Lake. Certainly Friday the 13th, May 1864, lived up to its name in these Virginia hills.

CHAPTER 14

Pollard Visits the Lake

After Crook's army passed, the neighboring people visited the lake to hunt for relics and pieces of equipment that might aid them on their farms. The area was an extremely dangerous border region. The hotel was probably only the resort of bushwhackers and dangerous mountain men. After the war an occasional stage brought the curious to see the lake and the site where a Union Army had camped. There was a stage stop and little else. However Mountain Lake was still a great tourist attraction. The stage line began to run again three times a week from Montgomery White Sulphur and Christiansburg. The Virginia and Tennessee Railroad ran through Christiansburg on to Central Depot or Radford, Dublin and Newbern. No railroad ran into Giles at this time.

In 1869 five years after Crook's men had visited the Lake one curious tourist who visited Mountain Lake was Edward Pollard of Richmond, the author of "The Virgina Tourist" who came to Montgomery County's White Sulphur and planned to go on to see the old "Salt Pond" one of the "sights of Virginia."

About travel to Eggleston and Mountain Lake Pollard said, "It is a pity that the place is so far removed from the railroad but there has recently been discovered a mode of access which we think far preferable to the stagecoach and of so inviting and romantic nature that Mr. Eggleston might advertize it as a new sensation for the tourist in Virginia."

What was this "new sensational" method of reaching Mountain Lake?

Take a boat!

"Leave the Virginia and Tennessee Railroad at New River bridge," says Pollard, "and float down the stream twenty-five miles in one of the batteaux which navigate it."

"The current of the stream takes the boat slowly down through a scenery most grand and picturesque upon which the eyes of the floating passenger may constantly feast."

"It is a journey," says Pollard, "that may be done in six or seven hours of daylight; and the batteau may be rigged with a shelter from the sun, and may be easily equipped with whatever comforts may be required. Some ladies from New Orleans had adopted this mode of reaching the springs. They had music on the water; there were wonders to tell of a scenery such as they had never seen before, a diorama of the banks of New River. They were enthusiastic in praises of the delightful and romantic conveyance which they had preferred to that ordinarily adopted by the traveler."

The lake was still considered mysterious and foreboding. Many looked on Mountain Lake as a giant basin from which the stopper might be pulled at any moment, sucking water and anyone upon it into the bowels of the earth. While at Montgomery White Sulphur Pollard heard a group discussing a visit to the lake.

"Some ladies there had planned a trip to Salt Pond escorted by gentlemen," says he.

An anxious mama made a gentleman promise that her daughter not be permitted to go in a boat out upon the lake.

When the gentleman protested that there was no danger the mama replied, "I don't know about that - it is a curious sort of thing that pond! If I was on it I should feel all the time as if the bottom might fall out!"

No matter what anyone said Pollard was determined he was going to see Mountain Lake. He said it was located on the "thoroughfare of the Springs Region of Virginia " and "in the neighborhood of this mysterious lake one may get glimpses of the matchless scenery of New River," said Pollard.

Although stages ran three times a week from Christiansburg pass Salt Pond to the springs of West Virginia Pollard decided not to take the stage. A companion mounted on a " horse beast" so called by the mountain people and Pollard on a mule jogged toward the lake. In Montgomery County they passed "broad acres of wide warm fields" with "groves in which stand the square houses of the country gentry of Virginia."

" Leaving Blacksburg a pretty village which boasts a `college' of some sort we were soon ascending Brush Mountain", Pollard notes. They headed for Eggleston Springs the new name for old Chapman's Springs. William Eggleston, now home from the war as Captain Eggleston, had bought the springs from the Mountain Lake company and had reopened it. Pollard planned to spend the night there.

"We have been told that the hotel accomodations at the Pond were vile beyond description," said Pollard.

They could hardly have been otherwise. Armies, one of them numbering nearly ten thousand, had literally overrun the hotel and camped around it. Runaway slaves and their families had camped on the grounds. Lawless bushwhackers had frequented the place. All had left behind their filth and debris. Certainly after four years of the most vicious war America has seen, Mountain Lake hotel and resort could have hardly been a pleasant place.

Eggleston Springs was still in good condition. Pollard claims that Eggleston was "the most delicious and comfortable of the resorts in the mountain section of Virginia."

"We would sup on broiled pheasant, drink the most famous of whisky toddies and go to sleep on the banks of the New River in view of Pomphey's Pillar and Caesar's Arch."

After spending the night at Eggleston they headed up the Doe Creek road, visited the old mill, and the Cascades finally arriving at the Salt Pond "hotel."

"Poverty and filth surround the place," Pollard related. "What is called a "hotel" we found to be a single dreary house built like a barn, the cattle housed under the front portico. A muddy scow pushed from the slime on the bank where it is rotting was the only conveyance we could get on the water. The large, bleak house, cut up into rooms, hotel-fashion, appeared to be deserted. It was only when we entered it that we were surprised to find a swarm of unsavory humanity hid away in it - men, women and children pigging together in the dirty rooms, and scarcely aroused to notice the appearance of strangers or to answer our questions except in sullen monosyllables"

It seems these were not local people but newcomers to Giles County. Pollard says, "An emigrant company of East Tennesseans had come to make a settlement here, and for the present inhabited the hotel. It was a dreary collection of the old and young of a people whom poverty had driven to new adventures in the wilderness. A pitiful, shrunken woman, a specimen of the "respectable" poor, entered into conversation with us. Warren asked her how she liked her new home. "It is a hard life," she replied,"but (with an air of superiority) what I mind most is that there is no society here."

Pollard said he was not ridiculing the woman for he felt the same way.

"A country where we may ride for miles without seeing a house, even a log cabin, where in the stillness of evening we may look from the road-side or the mountain over unbroken forests stretched to the stained sky and hear no sign of life - not the bark of a dog, not the tinkle of a bell - may give momentary emotions to the passing traveler (who) may exclaim"How grand is this solitude!" But to live in it, to bind up our life and work in such a scene, is a thought that appalls and in a moment the solitude has become changed and oppressive when we realize it no longer as a passing picture, but as an allotted home."

Though late in the day Pollard and friend decided to go up to Bald Knob and view the scenery. He said the stage line passed in sight of the Lake and just under the brow of Bald Knob.

"It was only half a mile farther to the mountain's summit, and we could go up on horseback."

He was glad he went.

"If I had not gone to Bald Knob I would have missed what by far most rewarded our journey, and I would not have my present reflections, that the finest view in Virginia is comparatively unknown and is yet to be advertized to the tourist."

He judged the top of the mountain to be about a thousand feet above the Lake. The summit he found to be a globular surface, a broken crown of rock to the north, some acres of dark soil thickly covered with undergrowth. "What appeared to be bushes a foot and a half high are really dwarfed oak trees, bearing acorns."

They could see a hundred miles in any direction. They could see into five states - Virginia, West Virginia, Kentucky, Tennessee and North Carolina.

" The wildness of it exceeded that of the Peaks of Otter,"

said Pollard. "The savage grandeur of mountain scenery was spread around us and lifted up to the sky. New River appeared as a silver thread."

As they breathlessly viewed this scenic grandeur "a great white cloud swept near us, looking like a flying ship. We were near enough to have thrown a stone into it."

Pollard's description in 1869 reminds us of the tales of the first English explorers in the New River Valley, Thomas Batts and Robert Fallam, who climbed, not Salt Pond, but some mountain height on New River near Salt Pond in September 1671. They wrote that they "saw a glimmering light as from water. We supposed there to be a great Bay."

Evidently they saw hanging clouds having the appearance of a ship's sail just as Pollard did.

Pollard and companion decided they must see the view from Bald Knob at sunrise so decided to risk staying in the dirty hotel.

"We asked only shelter of the Tennessee emigrants and that was given us in an apartment used for a wood-room, in which we fortunately had abundant materials for a good fire, grateful enough in the mountain atmosphere," says Pollard.

They did not risk any other amenities of the inn. "We had some biscuits and cold meats in our bag, and a thick traveling shawl spread on the floor with our satchels for pillows was sufficient for the little time we gave to sleep."

They were up very early and walked up to Bald Knob while still dark. "The fog hung below us, around us, a shipless sea - not an object discernible upon it but the summit of the Cumberland Mountains in the distance, looking like a thin rim of coast seen far away at sea. Presently the fog arose above this too and drowned it and we stood upon a single island under the hollow sky, in a vast solemn ocean - no sail upon it, no sound of water - a gray, limitless, breathless sea."

When the sun appeared burning away the mist Pollard said it was like the earth being created again. "The mountains arose, the valleys were spread out and garnished, the eternal rocks were planted and the river traced when at last the sunlight streamed in full joy over the scene."

Pollard was understandably much taken with the natural grandeur of the Salt Pond Mountain and lake though he thought little of the hotel. "Salt Pond is a great curiosity to the common traveler, and may be much more to the man of science. If an enterprising Yankee had hold of the place, a large and pleasant hotel would be built here, there would be the finest boating imaginable on the water, the delightful mountain air and the scenes it encases would invite hundreds of visitors."
Even as Pollard wrote this in his "The Virginia Tourist" an "enterprising Yankee" had his eyes on the property.

A black family traveling on the Salt Pond-Salt Sulphur Road traveled by tourist Pollard (Photo courtesy Martha Hesser)

The Bowling Alley beside the lake (Photo courtesy Martha Hesser)

General Herman Haupt inspecting Union Army railroad during the Civil War (Photo courtesy Library of Congress)

CASCADE FALLS AND AT THE SPRING.

CHAPTER 15

Haupt's Hotel

General Herman Haupt of Philadelphia, the engineer General in charge of railways for the Union Army during the recent war, had heard about Mountain Lake. In 1869 he was President of several railways and rapidly becoming wealthy but it is not clear exactly how he got the Mountain Lake property. General Haupt himself merely says he "got it by various turns of the wheel of fortune."

His son relates, "My father General Haupt purchased the Mountain Lake property in 1869." He purchased from the Mountain Lake Company and Henley Chapman's heirs.

The property bought by General Haupt consisted of one hundred and eighty thousand acres, two hundred and fourteen immediately around and including the lake and the hotel.
Haupt tells us, "I bought a dilapidated hotel and outbuildings used as a relay for horses on the stage route from Christiansburg to the Greenbrier White."

Haupt said he wanted "to enjoy this quiet retreat with his family so made the old building habitable and his family came to live there."

His family at this time consisted of his wife Cecilia and sons Jacob, Edward and Lewis.

No sooner however, had he taken possession than visitors began to pour in from near and far. According to Haupt's son these visitors were friends from the north who would come and stay all summer.

"As there was no other shelter for them for miles they would not be refused," Haupt rather helplessly remembers.

He had suddenly found himself with so many friends he realized he would have to do something.

So Herman Haupt the railroad builder built the second Mountain Lake Hotel. It was completed in 1875/76. An addition was made to the east end in 1887.

He also built additional cottages, dormitories, stables and mills.

Somehow along the way the guests began paying board probably due to the promptings of Mrs. Haupt. When the Giles County Clerk heard she had paying guests he told her she would have to purchase a hotel license for ten dollars. This decided Mrs. Haupt to go into business.

Mrs. Haupt remembering the filthy hotel her husband had bought and its monicker "Salt Pond Hotel" decided something had to be done. After all she was the wife of a Union General. If she was going to run a hotel in rather hostile rebel country and entertain northern friends the place needed a bit of dignity. "The Salt Pond Hotel" smacked too much of its former low repute. So Mrs. Haupt changed the name from "Salt Pond Hotel" to "Mountain Lake Hotel".

General Haupt was well known among both Union and Confederate top brass. He had been at West Point with Robert E.

Lee, George Meade and U.S. Grant. He had been in charge of Union railroads and bridge construction. He was the founder of the Southern Pacific Railway. He had friends and acquaintances across the breadth of America. As expected the first season the "Mountain Lake Hotel" was overrun, everyone coming to see General Haupt's new mountain resort. So many people arrived that they had to resort to mattresses made of straw to provide beds for everyone.

One satisfied customer, W. Hallett Phillips, a lawyer from Washington, D.C. says, "I spent my summers there from 1873 to 1882."

The lawyer was thrilled. He says, "I know of no summer resort in the country to compare with it in point of scenery and climate. You find there the rare combination of mountain and lake. Two fine mountain streams run through the property which afford great sport for the angler. Nowhere do you find greater grandeur, greater diversity. You find nature in all its wildness and original luxuriance."

And so the Haupt family kept guests at Mountain Lake during the summers from 1870 to 1890. Thus began the Haupt Era.

General Haupt's Hotel
About 1876 (Photo courtesy
Martha Hesser)

The Ramble, Cascades and
Bear Cliff (Photo courtesy
Martha Hesser)

BALD KNOB

The nobs hobnobbing on Bald Knob
(Photo courtesy Martha Hesser)

CHAPTER 16

Sites of Interest Near Mountain Lake

During the Haupt Era the mountaineous terrain was explored and natural beauty spots located. These places were given names and came to have special meaning to many visitors at Mountain Lake. Here follows a list of places discovered and named before 1900: Cecilia Springs, Barney's Wall, Minie Ball Hill, The Cascades, Little Stony Creek Glen, The Ramble, Big Roof, Bear Cliff, Butt Mountain Cliffs, Bald Knob, Prospect Rock, Sellars Spring and Shanty, John's Creek, Doe Creek, Big Stony Creek, Look Off Rock, Little Stony Creek Mill, and Doe Creek Mill.

Each place was unique in its own way and had been given a name as a distinct place in the area immediately around the lake. Further away were such places as Kire, Peter's Mountain and John's Creek Mountain but they were at a distance and might not be visited by tourists to the lake. These places near the lake will be described here as they are described in advertising brochures of Mountain Lake before 1900.

Cecilia Springs

General Herman Haupt's wife was named Cecilia and certainly these springs were named for her. The spring near the hotel supplied the hotel with icy cold water.

Minie Ball Hill

This site is marked by a National Park Service sign but is not right where the sign is. The site is on the right of the road after crossing the stream and extends up to the right.

The Ramble

A boat dock or landing place on the lake at the lower end of the lake. Two rocks on either side were favorite diving-off places. The Ramble was especially popular for it was featured in a number of early Mountain Lake brochures.

Little Stony Creek Glen

Little Stony Creek drains the front side of Salt Pond Mountain. The high steep sides of this creek make a glen covered with hemlock and rhododendron. At one time a foot bridge crossed this Glen. Also a road along it led to the Cascades. Little Stony also supplied the hotel table with trout.

The Cascades

The beautiful falls on Little Stony Creek which plunges 90 feet. This is five miles from the hotel. A road from the hotel went to the Cascades. This road, even its trace, is not open to the public today because it is on private property. Before 1900 carriages could be driven to within one-half miles of the Cascades "where the passenger alights and walks down the Glen of Little Stony" says an early brochure. "The drive is full of interest from the time the carriage leaves the hotel until it reaches Little Stony Creek."

There was at one time a rustic footbridge just below the Cascades.

The Cascades were advertized in early lake brochures as being the most beautiful falls in the Appalachians.

Bald Knob

Behind the hotel, 448 feet higher than the Lake stands Bald Knob from which can be seen a stupendous view. A path led to the Knob which is 3/8's mile from the hotel and only a few minutes walk and even invalids were able to take this walk. The view from Bald Knob takes in five states and a radius of one hundred miles.

Big Roof

East of the hotel and just off the path to Bald Knob one came to Big Roof a huge ledge of rock under which one could sit. At the top near Big Roof a spring bubbled right out of the mountain top.

Barney's Wall

Six miles from the hotel is a magnificent rocky precipice or wall of rock rising perpendicular for several hundred feet and extending along the mountain side for about 1/4 mile. It is reached on horseback by following the Cascade Road to Little Stony Creek, crossing it and along the trail leading up the Mountain slope. Barney's Wall is about four or five miles from the hotel and approximately three miles west of the Cascades. The rider is brought suddenly on the brink of this mighty precipice of stupendous grandeur. "For grandeur appalling Barney's Wall transcends all" so claims an early brochure. Today perhaps the easiest way to find this can be found by following the National Park Service Cascades road up the toward the Cascades and then turning off to the left.

Bear Cliff

Two miles eastward from the hotel near Little Stony Creek is Bear Hill which has among other features a rocky gorge with a cavernous opening which can be reached both on horseback and on foot known as Bear Cliff.

Butt Mountain Cliffs

These cliffs near the Cascades were once reached by the road from the lake around to Pacer's Gap which came near the Cascades. Little Stony Creek drains Butt Mountain. This is about ten miles from the hotel but well worth the trek for all of Pembroke and the New River Valley can be seen from Butt Mountain.

Prospect Rock

One mile west of the hotel we come to the edge of a rocky precipice. A nice walk from the hotel brings the curious to this spot from which can be seen the entire Valley of Giles, the village of Pembroke and the New River winding like a ribbon. Today this rock is near the present golf course.

Sellar's Spring and Shanty

Sometime before 1886 a hunter named Sellar had built a shanty beside a spring near Mountain Lake. From here he would go hunting. He had sores on his face and body and when he washed in the spring he found the sores would heal, itching cease. He washed his whole body in the water and was soon well. In December 1886 a boy named Hamilton R. Kirk was diagnosed as ill with spinal meningitis leaving him prostrate with liver and kidney disease. The doctors could not cure him and in June 1888 Dr. R. H. Hoge advised his father to try Sellar's Spring water. The father, James Kirk, carried it over the mountains in jugs and gave it to his son. In a few hours it caused painless urination and the boy began to improve and was regaining his health. Jonathan Nickline, a farmer living about three miles from the spring, had a child who could retain neither food nor water but after given Sellar's Spring water could do so. Dr. Hoge's sister-in-law was suffering from diabetes and her life was prolonged two years by using water from Sellar's Spring.

Dr. Hoge said, "There may be elements or combinations of elements that elude the chemist, yet have powerful and salutary effects in eradicating disease and Sellar's Spring water is of this character."

Since the water was on the Mountain Lake property General Haupt wanted to take advantage of it. There had not been any mineral springs at Mountain Lake so Haupt wanted to use it to draw more guests to the resort. He had Dr. Hoge write a recommendation for him. Hoge testified, "It acts mildly on both liver and kidneys, also relieving constipation. It's action is similar to John's Creek springs. I consider it better than John's Creek. I have used it myself and advised others to use it and have obtained good results. I think it has no equal in the state."

Haupt sent a sample to the University of Pennsylvania for analysis. It was found to be heavy in zinc, ferric and aluminum sulphates. Haupt then termed it an alum spring.

John's Creek

John's Creek drains the back of Salt Pond and John's Creek Mountain. Before 1900 it was full of mountain trout and a favorite haunt of Mountain Lake fishermen.

Doe Creek

Doe Creek is another creek that tumbles down the side of Doe Mountain into New River. Doe Creek comes very close to draining Mountain Lake but by a lucky stroke of nature does not. If it had the lake might not exist.

Big Stony Creek

Westward from Mountain Lake is Big Stony Creek. The Salt Sulphur turnpike crosses this stream, which fishermen from Mountain Lake frequented.

Doe Creek Mill

This mill on the Doe Creek road was passed by hacks and travelers as they made the eight mile climb from Eggleston Springs to the lake and was nearer the hotel than the Little Stony mill. The Doe Creek mill is gone today.

Little Stony Creek Mill

This mill was on top of Salt Pond Mountain on Little Stony Creek above the Cascades and was three miles from the hotel. It was more difficult to get to than the Doe Creek mill. A huge trench had been built by Haupt to carry the water of Little Stony to run this mill. All is gone today.

Look Off Rock

This lookout point is on Butt Mountain 4195 feet above sea level and can be reached by going down the Doe Creek road about a mile and then heading toward Butt Mountain. Perhaps it is best approached from the back side which would be to go to the top of Minie Ball Hill, turn left, follow the old trail and go back to Butt Mountain.

The Cascades could once be reached by a road from Mountain Lake Hotel (Photo courtesy Martha Hesser)

Haupt's Last Brochure 1889
(Photo courtesy Martha Hesser)

Chapter 17

The Haupt Era

Mountain Lake was blessed by Providence that it fell into the hands of Herman Haupt. He was an engineer and had much experience in building roads and railroads. His engineering expertise was of great advantage in organizing these rambling mountain acres into a resort that would become world famous.

Haupt began in 1870 by surveying the property to establish his boundaries. He says, "I surveyed with the aid of my son, Professor Haupt, the trails, roads and streams of the property and employed John S. Peck, County Surveyor, to resurvey the boundaries."

The line that Peck surveyed is today known as the Peck line at Mountain Lake.

Haupt built a graded road following the route of Little Stony Creek down the mountain and to the mill and Cascades. Mountain Lake was stocked with thousands of salmon, trout and catfish. A boat house was built and Pollard's vision of boating on the lake became a reality.

Haupt not only built a new hotel at the lake but began a number of cottages. The first cottage seems to be the Cecilia Cottage named for Mrs. Haupt and built near Cecilia Springs about 1870. Other cottages built shortly thereafter were the Thompson Cottage and the Stewart Cottage. Later Gordon Porterfield, a Giles County lawyer, built Porterfield House for his family. As time passed other cottages would be built at Mountain Lake but these are the earliest.

At this early period tourists had to disembark at Christiansburg. Gilbert Porterfield, son of Gordon, says, "During the years of the Haupt management of Mountain Lake, and before the New River branch of the Norfolk and Western Railroad was built, passengers for Mountain Lake, were taken off at Christiansburg, the stage coach brought the passengers to Mountain Lake, stopped over night there, and then went on to Salt Sulphur Springs in West Virginia, the next day. On the following day they would return to Mountain Lake and to Christiansburg and carry such passengers as were coming back from Salt Sulphur."

When Haupt decided to sell the resort in the late 1880's he wrote advertisements describing all he had done at the lake. He says there was an old hotel building with 25 rooms with water carried to the third floor by gravity. This indicates the luxuries he had installed in the dirty hotel that tourist Pollard had ridiculed and the effort he was making to upgrade the building. Water piped into the house, not to mention up to the third floor, was an absolute luxury. The majority of homes in the New River Valley below Salt Pond Mountain did not have running water in the house at this time.

Other buildings installed during the Haupt Era were the Brown House containing a store, laundry, 12 large rooms and an attic. This was behind the old hotel.

In addition to the cottages already mentioned Haupt had built the Old Maids Cottage with chapel and four chambers, the

Sweetbriar Cottage with two rooms and the Garden House with two rooms.

One of the dormitories Haupt built was called Stewart House with 24 rooms for males only.

For recreation he had built a boat and bath house, a bowling alley and billiard room.

In addition to these buildings Haupt also had a grist and sawmill run by a turbine on Little Stony Creek with three dwellings surrounding them including a log house and barns. The large barn was 75 x 40 feet with "very capacious mows".

There was a slaughter house, pig sty, chicken house, smokehouse, ice house, summer house, and walks immediately surrounding the hotel.

There was a carpenter shop, blacksmith shop and forge 30 x 40 feet.

There were six miles of new roads built and miles of stone and rail fences on the property.

By the late '80's Haupt had cleared about 10 percent of the whole area. He predicted that 75 percent of the land was capable of cultivation.

In the summer of 1884 a small steam yacht was built and run for the diversion of the guests.

Gilbert Porterfield who would later manage Mountain Lake Hotel says, "I remember as a boy I went to Mountain Lake with my family and one of the Haupt boys, Jacob, Had built a Steam Boat to run on the lake and take passengers around the lake. We went in the boat with him, which was propelled by steam, which was generated by a wood fire. Of course coal had not at that time become so general as a fuel."

The fame of the hotel spread. Guests arrived from all over America, from Italy, France, Germany, England and from as far away as the Hawaiian Islands. The Haupts had made a success of their venture. However General Haupt was an extremely busy businessman and engineer. In addition to his work for the Southern Pacific he supervised construction of the Pennsylvania railway from Harrisburg to Pittsburg. He opened the Hoosaic Tunnel in Massachusetts and from 1883-1884 was the manager of the Northern Pacific at St. Paul, Minnesota.

Gilbert Porterfield says, "The Haupts, I think, must have taken on age and got tired of operating Mountain Lake."

Haupt simply did not have time to run a hotel and resort!

In 1888 Haupt wrote an advertising brochure and distributed it hoping to get a wealthy buyer - probably among his northern friends. Nothing came of the advertising. He realized he would have to throw in other inducements to attract buyers. So in 1889 he had Harry Norris come up to Mountain Lake to assess its resources.

Norris says, "After spending several weeks in examining the various resources at Mountain Lake I will say that iron and manganese are apparently unlimited. White and yellow pine in two considerable bodies are located on Big Stony. Sixty percent of the property could be converted into the very best farming and grazing land. The soil is exceedingly rich. Cereals and all products of the garden have been raised and the products have been almost phenomenal. Of the 40 percent of the land capable of farming and grazing quite a large proportion is taken up with mineral deposits and the remainder is mountaineous and worthless."

In January 1889 they had the result of an analysis of the water from the Alum Spring at Sellars Shanty on Big Stony.

Meanwhile the Norfolk and Western Railway had been building the railroad along New River into West Virginia. In 1889 they opened the station at Staytide opposite present Eggleston. From here travelers were brought to the summit of Salt Pond about a distance of eight miles in hacks supplied by the Mountain Lake Hotel. Haupt loudly proclaimed the ease with which you could come to Mountain Lake from any northern or southern city by the way of the Norfolk and Western.

Haupt was hoping to find some wealthy northerner like himself who would lavish money and time on the resort. But he was unable to do so. After several years on the market Mountain Lake was still not sold to that will-o-the-wisp wealthy Yankee.

Though he said he would not open again in 1889 he did. In his brochure for that season he describes further about the metals that had been found on the property. The results of analysis were "extremely gratifying". Ores were in much greater quantity than had been expected. Some samples for iron ore ran as high as 59 percent of metallic ore. Chemists J. Blodget Brittain and Prof. F.E. Genth ran the analyses.

Professor Genth ran an analysis of a springs about eight miles from the hotel. It was found to possess large quantities of salts of nickel, salts of zinc, copper, iron, magnesium, sodium, potassium and manganese. Genth said it was mine water rather than mineral water. Haupt said, "If nickel, zinc and copper should be found in quantities much additional value would be given the property."

Haupt did say that he would welcome all visitors for the 1889 season but it would be "the last under the present management."

From his 1889 brochure we gain further insight into the operation of Mountain Lake resort. He says that charges at the hotel are only about half as high as at hotels in other localities which remain open all year. No expense had been spared to get good food for the table. An agent with horse and wagon was employed constantly to travel through the neighboring valley to collect poultry, eggs and butter. Milk and cream were supplied from the hotel dairy and lambs, sheep and beeves are fattened on the mountain pastures.

"The absence of a bar has relieved Mountain Lake from a very unwelcome class of patrons and secured for it others whose presence is far more desirable," says the brochure.

Parents were to keep children under control and not permit racing in the halls or porches. They would not be permitted to use the boats unattended. There was swimming available but everyone was expected to bring their own bathing suit.

Detached building and cottages were connected with the hotel by board walks. As for rates - guests who remained for eight weeks would be charged the lowest rates for rooms occupied the whole time. Bills would be presented on the last day of each month. Transient rates for less than a week's stay were $2.00 to $2.50 daily.

It appears that Haupt was true to his word and did not return in 1890 but that W.E. Ragsdale became manager. He proposed to purchase with a plan to tear down Haupt's Hotel and replace it with a grand hotel three stories high and costing $40,000.00. Ragsdale's prospectus shows a Queen Anne style hotel with palm trees at the lake's edge. One winter at Mountain Lake frozen over with thick ice disrupted plans of palms trees and a Florida type resort. Nothing came of Ragsdale's plan.

Coal was becoming popular as a fuel. Land speculators began buying great tracts of mountain land in Virginia and West Virginia. The mineral analysis that Haupt had ordered now paid dividends. The possibility of valuable ores under the vast acreage around the lake made the property very attractive. Mountain Lake was suddenly valuable - not for the resort, or the timber, or the grazing land or the alum spring but for the ore or coal that might lie somewhere under the rambling acres. A company called the Mountain Lake Land Company with Frank Woodman of Charleston, West Virginia, as President, bought Mountain Lake from the Haupts in 1891. This company would in turn sell the resort property to Gordon Porterfield.

Ragsdale's Proposed Mountain Lake Hotel
about 1890 (Photo courtesy Martha Hesser)

David Blossom, (right) head man at Mountain
Lake Hotel with waiter believed to be Flem
Jackson (Photo courtesy Martha Hesser)

Gordon Porterfield, wife and children. Elder son, Gilbert, standing behind his father would manage the hotel about 25 years (Photo courtesy Robert Farrier)

CHAPTER 18

The Porterfield Management

Since the Gordon Porterfield family were to become the owners of the resort and play such a prominent role in the history of Mountain Lake Resort we will let one of them tell us of the transaction from the Haupts to them.

Gilbert Porterfield writes, "During the last years of the 19th century, Mountain Lake was purchased by the Mountain Lake Land Company from the Haupts and along with this purchase, they acquired several thousand acres of mountain land surrounding Mountain Lake which ran into West Virginia. About that time my father had become a practicing Attorney and he was Attorney for the Mountain Lake Land Company with Mr. Frank Woodman of Charleston, West Virginia, as its President. Of course Mr. Woodman did not want to operate Mountain Lake as a resort so my father made a deal with him for the purchase of the Resort property with 2500 acres of land surrounding the Resort Hotel. It was then that he became the Manager of the then new Resort, when I was just a boy still. I had not completed my schooling for I was at that time attending the National Business College of Roanoke and I would visit my family at Mountain Lake during the summer time. My father had associated with him several people around the county."

Gordon organized a company called the Mountain Lake Hotel Company with himself as President, T. A. Taylor as Vice-President and Manager, and Martin P. Farrier as Secretary. "Gord" as Porterfield was called, attempted to manage the resort in the years of 1891-1894. Martin Farrier was also a busy lawyer and these two lawyers realized they needed full time managers. By 1895 T.A. Taylor was full-time manager with F.E. Dunklee as a clerk. Soon he would become manager.

A young schoolteacher named Bierne Ellison had recently come to Giles from Lowell, West Virginia, to teach a one-room school for Charles F. Tinsley who had a wagon and carriage works at Hoge's Store. Tinsley repaired hacks and kept them in running order as they passed his place on the eight mile climb up to Mountain Lake. Tinsley was a crusty fellow once threatening to take Ellison's schoolhouse keys because he remarked that postage stamp revenue supported the schools. When Ellison was not teaching and short on money he wanted to sell his horse and Tinsley told him Dunklee at Mountain Lake might buy the horse. Tinsley knew the Porterfields needed new horses to outfit the hack service and livery at the hotel. So Ellison went up to the lake and was given a job as clerk in 1895. He would become manager later and remain at Mountain Lake Hotel until 1912 when he left to manage the Dining Hall at Virginia Tech. Whether his horse ever ended up pulling a hack up and down Salt Pond Mountain we know not.

The Porterfields had printed up nice new brochures. In the Mountain Lake brochure for 1895 they explain, "We have leased Mountain Lake, the most delightful of all Virginia's Mountain Resorts, for the season of 1895. Our experience with the wants and tastes of all that desire to spend the summer pleasantly in the mountains and who wish to recuperate their wasted strength resulting from disease or overwork enables us to make our guests comfortable."

"It was generally conceded last summer by our visitors that no better table was kept in Virginia than was found at Mountain Lake. We are determined it shall not fall below the reputation it has enjoyed but shall be even better."

They promised that the rooms will have "new mattings, carpets and curtains".

"We have also built a number of new cottages which cluster around the lake and main buildings." The historian has no way of knowing which cottages were built by the Porterfield management before 1900.

They advertize the hotel as having "one hundred and twenty rooms with a large and spacious dining room, elegant ladies' parlor, hot and cold baths which afford ever comfort that can be found in a metropolitan hotel. Around the entire front of the hotel are two broad piazzas, one above the other, the most lovely promendade in Virginia."

The mail ran daily and the hotel was lighted with gas, had a steam laundry and all modern improvements.

As for the roads up to the lake they promise, "All roads leading to Mountain Lake will be kept in much better condition for vehicles and for horseback riding than before. Ladies expecting to be much on horseback will bring with them their side saddles and riding habits."

The rates per month were $40.00 to $45.00; weekly they were $12.00 to $15.00 and daily $2.00 to $2.50. These charges included room, lights and servants' attention. Children and nurses taking their meals in the children's ordinary will be charged half the above rates. There would be an extra charge for milk provided for infants.

The season opened June 1 but parties coming earlier would find good accomodations.

And it had become easy to reach Mountain Lake by rail. The Norfolk and Western sold summer excursion tickets to Pembroke which was the nearest and most convenient station to Mountain Lake. Other rail lines were selling tickets to Eggleston Springs and a special arrangement had been made that people using these tickets could be taken on to Pembroke at no extra charge.
When the tourist was deposited at Pembroke how was he or she to find their way to Mountain Lake?

The Mountain Lake Hotel Company owned a hack line from the Pembroke Station to Mountain Lake and also livery at the lake. The 1895 brochure said the livery was all new - horses, hacks and buggies, the best to be found in the state.

Guests were supposed to notify the Mountain Lake hotel of

their expected time of arrival so the hack could be waiting.

It is interesting to see the cost of hiring a hack in these last years of the 19th century at Mountain Lake.

Fare from Pembroke to the lake was $1.25; ferriage and one trunk was free. The use of one horse one hour was .75; two or three hours $1.25 and one day $2.50. A trip to the Cascades and back in the hack could be made for $1.00. It must be recalled that there was a road at that time from the hotel to the Cascades.

Amusements included boatriding, fishing, lawn tennis, bowling, dancing, horseback riding, buggy riding, music and swings.

"A supply of elegant boats will be kept on the lake at a nominal cost. The lake was never fuller than this year. Fifteen to twenty springs empty into it breaking out from the adjacent mountain side. Numerous springs in the lake all give a never ending supply of water. So announces the 1895 brochure.

The Porterfield management advertized their lake and resort as 4500 feet above the level of the sea at the south end of a plateau situated almost at the summit of one of the highest mountains in Virginia.

" Near the lake is Bald Knob rising 448 feet higher than the lake. From it is one of the finest views in the entire Allegheny range. The lake is fringed nearly its entire circumference with a dense growth of rhododendrons... giving a border of unsurpassing beauty. Five miles from the hotel is the Glen of Little Stony Creek from which "leaps the most beautiful cascade yet found in the mountains of Virginia."

"Wherever one saunters in the woods he finds the ground covered with an inpenetrable mass of giant ferns and sees the greatest variety of mountain flowers, some delicately tinted, some brilliantly colored. Anyone desiring to look upon mountain scenery in all its beauty and grandeur, to gaze upon an almost endless alteration of hill and dale, valley and mountain, rivulet and lake, should not fail to visit Mountain Lake."

These splendid verbal flourishes usher in the Porterfield era at Mountain Lake.

In the spring of 1897 the lake resort was being readied for the guests that would soon be coming when an unusual physical phenomena occurred. The second largest earthquake ever known in the southeastern United States hit Giles on May 31. A story is told concerning this event by the author's grandmother, Josephine Williams Porterfield, who lived with her husband and children on a farm at the foot of John's Creek Mountain near where route 700 or the present Mountain Lake road comes down near Sinking Creek. One night the family were all asleep but Josephine happened to be awake when she suddenly heard an extremely loud whistling sound or bugling which permeated the house filling the air with its sound. Thinking an oil lamp had been left on and was ready to explode she jumped up and raced from room to room and downstairs and back up but found only her sleeping family. As suddenly as it had come the noise ceased. Shortly thereafter the Giles earthquake occurred and scientists today say that high pressure steam precedes earthquakes which makes a whistling sound as it finds its way through rocks or caves toward the surface. Grandmother probably heard escaping high pressure steam issuing from a nearby cave (Tawney's Cave has a little known entrance on this farm).

This quake was a 5.8 quake and shook everybody up considerably. Reports were out that Angel's Rest had split and that Mountain Lake had split wide open. People rushed up to the lake to see but Mountain Lake was just the same - its waters twinkling and sparkling as always. A telegram was sent from Giles County that Mountain Lake was still intact. This was published in the Richmond Dispatch on June 4 which reported "for a week or more before the shock people throughout Giles County were much disturbed by subterranean noises and all day Monday detonations like the explosion of distant artillery were heard". On June 4 the same newspaper reported "if the buildings throughout Giles had been largely of brick, the damage would have been very great and serious loss of life would have occurred." There were "four separate shocks on May 31st between 2 and 5 o'clock p.m."
Mr. Sam May an attorney was in Pearisburg trying a case and said "the quake was really severe. Some thought Mountain Lake had caved in. I think the water did go down some but if there was a crack in the bottom it evidently filled up gradually."
Just afterwards people were afraid of going to the lake but gradually curiosity got the better of them and they went up. The 1897 season was especially successful for everyone had something new to talk about.

The hotel when the Porterfield management began (Photo courtesy Martha Hesser)

The lake was very full in 1896 when this picture was made before the earthquake (Photo courtesy Martha Hesser)

Mountain Lake several years after the earthquake shows a reduced water level (Photo courtesy Martha Hesser)

When the railroad came Castle Rock Ferry was where tourists crossed the New River on the journey to Mountain Lake (Photo courtesy Martha Hesser)

Mountain Lake Hotel hack crossing New River on the ferry at Castle Rock 1895 (Photo courtesy Martha Hesser)

CHAPTER 19

The Mormon Church at Mountain Lake

In 1898 a new development occurred at Mountain Lake. A Mormon church was founded there among the people who worked at the resort. During the summer these people were busy at the hotel but in the winter it was a place of great loneliness and isolation. When Mormon missionaries traveling through from Salt Sulphur found the little settlement they found a willing audience.

Mormon elders had been in Giles County as early as 1844 when Elders Daniel Carter, Pitts and Biles and Elders Joseph King and Alfred Lambson were preaching in the area. Elder King had been at the General Conference in Nauvoo in spring 1844 and heard the Mormon prophet Joseph Smith speak shortly before he was assassinated. Immediately after that event Elder King writes that he felt the missionaries in Giles County should return to Nauvoo and aid in the exodus of the Mormons to the far west.

There followed the long trek of the Mormons to the Great Salt Lake Valley where all their energies were concentrated on settling the desolate Rocky Mountain regions. It was only in 1897 that they sent missionaries back to Giles county. In 1897 Elders A.A. Day and Orin W. Jarvis were in Pearisburg and apparently were the elders who found the Mountain Lake settlement. In April 1898 Elder Thomas C. Romney and Benjamin Walker organized the Mountain Lake Sunday School composed of twenty people. Twelve of these gave their address as Mountain Lake while the rest gave Newport as their post office. From this handful of people has grown congregations of Latter-Day Saints numbering in the thousands.

It can be said that the Church of Jesus Christ of Latter-Day Saints in the Middle New River Valley was founded at Mountain Lake.

The first convert of the Mormon elders at Mountain Lake was a man named Joseph Smith, born July 4, 1847, at Newport, the child of John Smith and Mildred Ann Harless. He was baptized by Elder Day on February 27, 1898. His wife Emma L. Smith, daughter of Charles C. Porterfield and Margaret E. Price was baptized March 2, 1898.

Joseph and Emma Smith were the first converts at Mountain Lake. It was coincidental that they bore the names of the first Mormon prophet Joseph Smith and his wife, Emma and that they lived by a "Salt Lake in the Mountains" just as the Mormons in Utah lived by a Salt Lake in the mountains.

The next convert was Charles E. Smith son of Gaspar Link Smith and Mary O. Songer and his wife Lucy Smith, daughter of Joseph Meredith and Helen Martin. The next converts were Gasper Link Smith, son of John Smith and Mildred Ann Harless, and his wife Mildred, daughter of Abraham Harless and Catherine Link; Mary Olvey Smith, daughter of Francis Marion Songer and Susie Ann Louks (Lucas), John Smith son of John Smith and Fannie Rains, Laura Lou Smith, daughter of John Pike and Ada Collins. Then followed baptism in June 1899 of the children of Elizabeth Kirk,

William Everett, Maybellie, Fannie Susan and Stewart Harvey. Martha Louise Kirk, child of James Kirk and Frances Martin, Annie Missouri Collins, daughter of Henley Collins and Emily Williams, Louisa Anna Smith, daughter of John Smith Jr. and Nancy Rhoda Wood were next converts. Minnie Arabell Smith, daughter of Harvey Green Smith and Laura L. Pike, Lettie Williams, daughter of John Farley and Aggie Lucas, Virginia P. Smith daughter of James W. Martin and Mary A. White joined Paris Taylor, son of James and Parthenia Taylor, for baptism in 1900.

Other members of the above families later joined the Mormon group at Mountain Lake.

From this small Sunday School organized in a blacksmith-carpentry shop at Mountain Lake has come many congregations of the Mormon Church in the surrounding area in Virginia and West Virginia. Other Mormon groups organized in 1898 and 1899 in Virginia have long since vanished. But the Mountain Lake Sunday School flourished and grew just as the mountain flowers that bloomed about it. The descendants of these people are strewn throughout the area. Missionaries have gone from them to all parts of the globe. When Mormon missionaries came to Joseph and Emma Smith living by their Mountain Lake at the end of the century in 1897 they found as fertile a field for cultivation as botanists Pursch or Lyon found at the beginning of the century when searching for wild flowers.

CASCADE GLEN AND BALD KNOB.

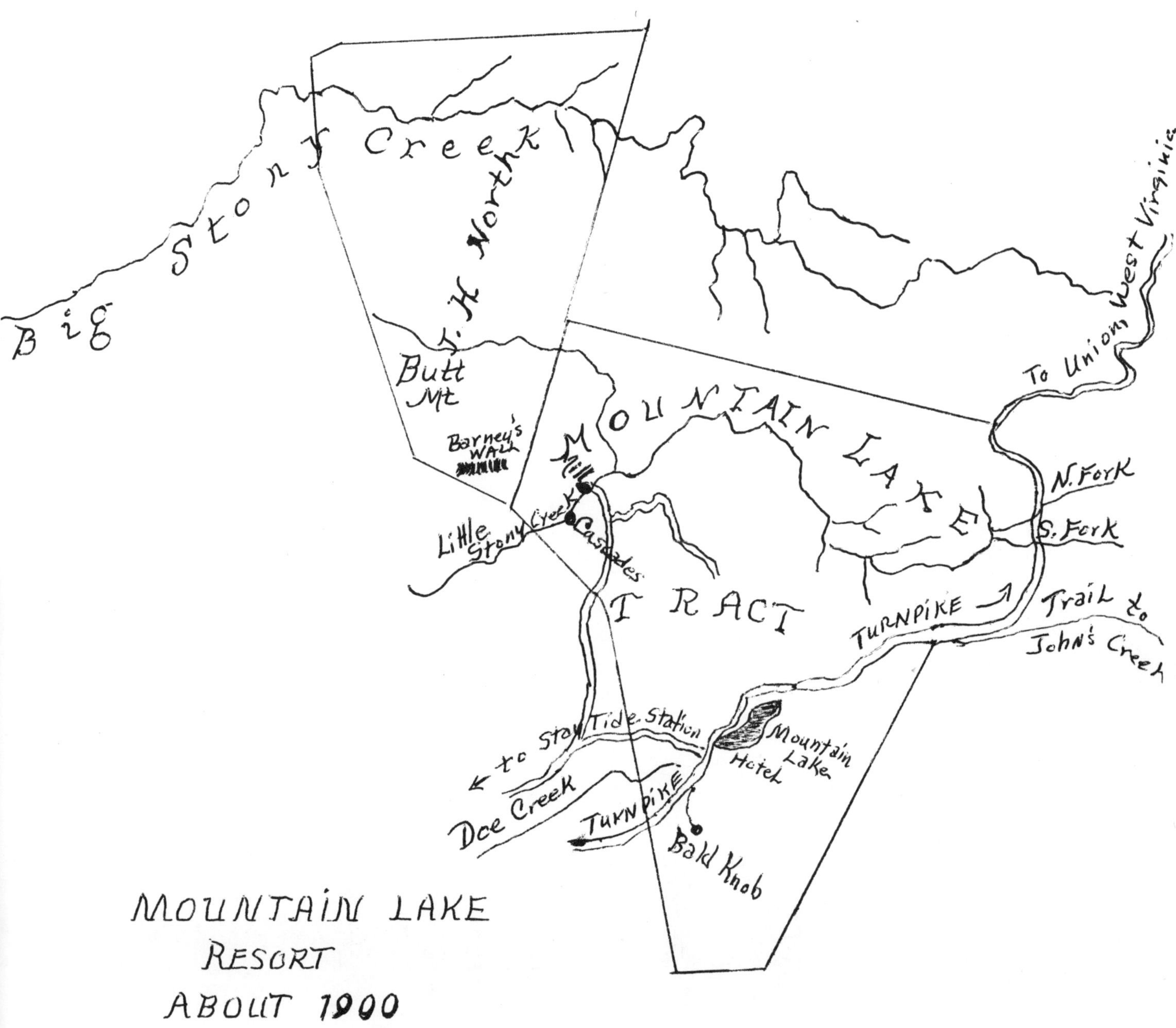

MOUNTAIN LAKE
RESORT
ABOUT 1900

Craig County Party of McPhersons,
Reynolds, Givens and Ellisons
at Mountain Lake about 1899
(Photo courtesy Virginia Price Givens)

Fishing about 1900 (Photo courtesy
Martha Hesser)

CHAPTER 20

A New Century Begins at Mountain Lake

The fame of the resort continued to grow. By the century's end the Mountain Lake Hotel Company headed by Gordon Porterfield was firmly in control and their good management was widely advertised. The resort drew crowds. The crush of people season after season caused wear and tear. Repairs constantly had to be made in the fall and winter months after the guests had gone. As seen a small community of white people who tended the hotel were always on hand. Also not far from the hotel along the road down to Newport had grown up a tiny settlement of negroes most of whom worked at the hotel. One of these was David Blossom, the head waiter at the hotel. Among these whites and negros there were carpenters and craftsmen and they made the repairs around the resort. Sometimes local craftsmen from Newport or Pembroke would also come up to the lake to make repairs and new additions.
In 1899 the hotel company spent $3,500.00 in improvements. Due to these repairs and a brisker management the hotel was now able to open earlier. The 1900 season opened May 1 but would accept guests even before that date.

Mountain Lake was now being advertized as the "Silver Gem of the Alleghenies". The brochures for that year carried all the same claims as to the lake's beauty, how the banks were lined with rhododendron, laurel and azalia. It was mentioned that it was fed entirely by springs but had an outlet the waters of which flowed into Little Stony Creek.

The resort was proclaimed "The Eldorado of the Sportsman and the Ponce de Leon of the Invalid".

"Here the tired overworked businessman may rest and the sportsman find his recreation. Bears can be found on Little Stony Creek. The lake is well stocked with California trout, a fact not known until three years ago. Nearby Little Stony Creek, Big Stony and John's Creek abound in mountain trout. The hotel tables in fact are supplied with these mountain trout." So proclaims the 1900 Mountain Lake brochure.

Virginia Price Givens tells of her father hunting on Mountain Lake Mountain at this time before the turn of the century.

"Around Mountain Lake area the bears and the foxes were killing the lambs and the sheep and even the calves and fowls. The deer were destroying the crops. At this time about eight or ten men formed a hunting party which lasted several days at a time. There is a nice cave near Mt. Lake where the men slept, it was wide in the middle and sloped to each end so the tall men slept in the middle and the short men at the ends. On one trip during a severe drought they failed to find water but they had plenty of food. One hunter, Mr. John Alf Brewer, declared that he could not eat without washing his face as he never had done such a thing. But the others pitched in full force and their only regret was the lack of water for hot coffee. Two of their much loved hounds were Music and Smoky. Smoky had earned his name by running so fast through the mountain that he merely looked like smoke. And here let us drink in the rare and melodious notes of "Old Music."

Mrs. Givens continues by naming "those who belonged to the hunting party were Uncle Will Price, Uncle Sam Hoge, Mr. John Hoge, Mr. John Alf Brewer and Uncle Albert Price."

Boating was now coming into its heyday at Mountain Lake. The hotel management had gotten new boats and advertized their boats hastening to add that "boating is very safe." This was to counter all the past gossip about the deadly depths of the lake - how ghostly trees stood in the bottom - how the lake might someday be sucked right into the bowels of the mountain. And it was the future that held the tragic drownings that occurred when people fell out of boats.

And so began a new century at Mountain Lake. To usher in this century we will go on a camping party to the lake as recorded by the chaperone.

CHAPTER 21

The Mountain Lake Camping Party

In this summer of 1900 a large group from Radford outfitted by Colonel Warner Kinderdine left Radford to spend a week at Mountain Lake. Kinderdine had come to Radford during the railroad boom and was financially able to outfit a wagon of young people on a week-long trip to Mountain Lake. A journal was kept by the chaperone of the party of this trek to the lake. Fifteen people were in the party. They were the following.

1. Mr. Chicken (Radford Adams?)
2. Mr. Dependable-Boy Billee (William Ingles?)
3. The Soldier (?)
4. Hannah the Blond (Hannah Washington?)
5. Hannah Brune (The Second Hannah?)
6. William Kurtz
7. The Nurse (?)
8. Anna Kinderdine (Daughter of Colonel Kinderdine)
9. Atchley Tinsley (Tinsley from Hoge's Store?)
10. Jean?
11. The Widow?
12. Mr. Hearon
13. Mr. Adams (Putnam Adams?)
14. The Chaperone (Mrs. Warner Kinderdine?)
15. Uncle Milton Turner, driver of the wagon. He had been a boy slave of Dr. John Blair Radford and after emancipation hired out to the Radford and Adams families.

The Mountain Lake Camping Party

by The Chaperone

On Monday August 20th 1900 old Sol looked over the rim of Radford upon a moving sight. The wagons, one overflowing with humanity, the other with all modern conveniences, and viands fit for the Gods, rolled down First Street causing the spectators to weep great green tears of envy and to kick themselves for having come out on that particular morning, ahunting the early worm. The settling process in wagon No.1 occupied several miles. At last the Chicken crowly gaily on the front seat beside the Dependable young man - Boy Billee, after a struggle with opposing forces found a resting place for his pedal extremities. The Soldier flourished the guns and armed himself to the the teeth. The girls fitting in like bread in a lunch basket, two slices to each sandwich. The wayside people stopped to gaze in admiration at the flower garden of hats that met their astonished gaze for the wagon fluttered with brilliancy of orange, crimson, green, snowwhite, pink, red-white and blue hat strings and one frivolous thing in black chiffon. In the rear of the wagon with one strong eye fixed immovably upon each row of giddy campers, sat the chaperone - and through all that transpired - whether "hair breadth scapes by field or flow" - those eyes neither quivered

Camping on the Mountain Lake Trip
Uncle Milton Turner who drove the wagon at far right (Photo courtesy Minnie Fitting)

Radford Adams leaning against the wagon as they prepare to leave Radford on the Mountain Lake Trip (Photo courtesy Minnie Fitting)

nor slept. Merrily we bumped along, smiling so pleasantly upon all we met that those unfortunates invariably contracted the "mean guns" and hated themselves for not having turned aside before encountering so much beatitude. Twice the wagons were ferried across New River which glides with golden, snakelike undulations through the sweet, green country while above, the sun rode forth upon his fiery steeds, with a specially warm smile for the Radford Party - and on we bumped.

Just after Dependable with his usual unerring judgment, had selected one of Prices historic Forkes, the Chaperone, happening to glance upward, detected a wicked smile upon Ancient Sols beaming countenance moreover, he winked at Her with his left eye. She beheld him deliberately dart forth one of his beams, and draw towards him a fat, black cloud. The next minute the graceful draperies of the wagon descended and the party had their first experience under canvass. After this practical joke had been played and had failed to dampen either hats or spirits, the caravan entered the streets of Blacksburg, famed for being the incubator of the Chicken's intellectual life. In delicate consideration for the quality of the reputation this worthy fowl gave us to understand he established in town, we deemed it best for all parties to step quietly through the streets and so cast anchor a mile and a half beyond, at the truly hospitable home of Miss Keister and Mrs. Wilson. Long will these ladies be remembered with real pleasure by our party. Lunch - and what a Lunch! (The boys said it was equal to anything they had ever eaten at Delmonicos) It was spread upon a bench on the porch. After a full enjoyment of the delicacies a majority of the girls went within to wash faces, repair pompadours and to take reefs in their skirts, but Hannah the Blond, who though on pleasure but ever preserves a frugal mind, laid in a fresh supply of apples and tomatoes.

At last we were aboard again and all jolted merrily until we reached the innocent looking village of Newport. Nothing warned us of a lurking danger. In the unblinking gaze of the grocery store gentry we detect no guile. Under the very shadow of a great coming event, we looked with levity upon the doctor, lawyer and the drug clerk sunning themselves upon the hotel porch & in their midst was a Presence whose exterior was that of other men, and gave no hint of an unlawful familiarity with spirits of the mountain fiery and strong.

The Chaperone by this time, softened beyond doubt by the bumps smiled encouragingly upon the exuberance of the young folks and even raised in unison with their voices, a discreet cheer for Radford. she afterward admitted that she detected and frowned not, certain smiles and glances that flashed out from a triangle formed by a black pompadour and two orange bonnet strings, and that winged their lightning way towards the porch - where lurked the Presence. A glance and a smile are impalpable trifles - mere moonshine - and yet moonshine may produce palpable effect. The Radford Camping-party can testify to the truth of this logic. And now the wagons have reached an ideal spot. In a green cup between tall hills nestles Porterfield's farm and over it all broods the spirit of Peace, at least we thought so. So we one accord called it Peaceful Valley though before leaving we changed its name to Shooting Creek. In pitching the tents Mr. Kurtz and the "Chicken" vied with each other in feats of industry. The girls meanwhile repaired to the house to forage, the trained nurse, having the most "taking way" with the People, was elected leader of the expedition which was successful beyond our hungriest expectations. It was at this juncture that the masculines made impertinent enquiries into the state of the larder resulting in a predicted meat famine and causing a panic which being entirely without foundation, ruffled exceedingly the calm of the less carnal sex. But they were equal to the emergency each in her own peculiar way. A band of the most earnest still led by the nurse entered into a dark conspiracy with a native young man for the secret purchase and delivery of a ham. It has never been clearly determined whether the ham or the impalpable smile and glance at Newport brought about the awful climax to which this narration is rushing. While the ham conspirators conspired in dusky corners in whispers sweet, Hannah the Blond walked openly in the sun gathering large stores of apples and tomatoes reminding all that a vegetable diet, particularly acid varieties, was the most wholesome for camping parties. A splendid hot supper, the memory of which made us sweetly sad just a week later on the same spot, was followed by a visit from Mrs. Manus of the Porterfield's Mansion. This lady is a mono-maniac on the subject of Payne genealogy but caught in a lucid interval, she regaled us with one or two thrilling moonshine stories. When she had departed watermelons were eaten and goodnights said, and at last the party was aslep under canvas, grand sensation! We had hardly gotten used to the novelty before we were sweetly, soundly sleeping. It was a crashing clap of Thunder that roused us from dreams of home to the realization of camp life in a storm. The rain on a tent is not quite so musical as it is on a roof. Each one lying on her bed raised a hand and touched the canvas to see if it was wet through. A strange thing happened: a little crystal stream followed each finger tip, and we stirred uneasily in our downy nests. We did considerable talking for the rest of the night and in the morning added rubber shoes to our house toilets. In the other tent which was shaped like the letter A with sides and no ends there arose some slight unpleasantness among the inmates. The Chicken with characteristic dread of water, conceived the idea that the tent was about to blow away. Frantically assuming his feathers, he both by precept and example endeavored to force his tent fellows to do like wise. The Dependable Gentleman is no doubt slanderously accused of having used "languages". Daylight found the rain coming down in a steady business like drizzle and the Dependable decided that no stakes should be pulled that day. At this autocratic mandate the ladies who had breathed "Excelsior" at every turn of the wheels almost fell into meeting but the Chaperone throwing herself into the widening breach endeavored and successfully out of the superabundance of her confidence and appreciation, to again inspire perfect party faith

in the discernment of our Leader. And so we settled happily for a day and night in Camp Jean. (The Porterfield Farm?)
Charades occupied the morning hours. Miss Anna Kinderdine and Mr. William Kurtz being star actors. At last the shades of night enveloped the vale and what happened twixt Sun and Sun in that deceitful Valley is fairly tattoed upon the memories of our Camping party especially Hannah Brune and so this humble member of the expedition, honored as she is by her election to the position of Chief Recorder, forbears to tamely recount, in the mild vocubulary at her command, the harrowing incidents of that never to be forgotten night. Suffice to say that Mr. Rosenfeld distinguished himself for prudence under provocation, the Solder went gallantly into action. Mr. Kurtz as ever faithful to the ladies won the Sobriquet of the Defender, and as for the Dependable, where would we be now, but for his wisdom and his guile? Like the Kildee that gaily leadith the enemy from her nestlings, so the Dependable carried off the desperadoes, and feigned a wild carouse with them in their own parlor. But alas! as so often happens in this thankless world, his disinterested and useful conduct was misinterpreted and unappreciated for in an election which followed soon after he was defeated by Mr. Kurtz, showing plainly that he had nursed a whole nest of vipers at his camp fireside. It must also be recorded that the songful cork and Indian guide made faithful sentinels on that fateful night and that the girls were all heroines Hannah Brune, it is true expressed in act and word a strong abhorrence of filling a grave that night besprinkled with mountain dew and steeped in moonshine, but the soldier vigorously reassured and comforted her there by proving that "the bravest are the tenderest". It was edifying to behold the celerity with which the stakes were pulled and tents folded the next morning for once the masculines had an uninterrupted job, for the ladies lent their fair hands to the work. Up the mountain at last! Short pulls and short rests, and Oh! what views between the trees! Words cannot paint them and only those who have seen can realize. It was half past one one Wednesday when the two wagons drew up near the Mountain Lake Hotel.

Gypsies, the people thought and stared, and the party was not sorry when the wagons started again on the last joltest stage to the camping ground. How snug our gentlemen made us in camp will ever be a pleasant memory. The kitchen with stove and dressers aglitter with tomato cans, tin basins, etc. The Summer dining room with an arched roof frescoed in blue and white wall hung with forest green and a violet carpet of tender green ferns on a brown ground. But best of all was the ladies tent with the real Brussels carpet, its twelve foot bedstead and cots, its dressing table and mammoth mirror, the result of the vanity of three fourths of the party and of the patient endurance and muscle of the whole. Summing up the comforts and conveniences of this tent were too numerous to mention. As for the gentleman's domicile, I am reliably informed (Mr. Chicken being my authority) that they had a chiffonier and no doubt everything else in keeping. How can I ever attempt to describe life at Camp Fernwood? This effort is only intended as a memoranda, from which on future darker days, we may call forth the treasured memories of this happy week, set like jewels in nature's most beautiful handiwork the mountain scenery of Mountain Lake. Too freshly remembered now are the jokes, the sentimental passages (which the Chaperone neither saw or even suspected), the merry meals, the sunsets and rises on the Knob, the floating on the Lake and the splashing in it. And then too the Widow - our own particular widow "fashioned as tenderly young and so fair"! A subject to be handled with care for we discerning feminines do truly believe that every unfortified masculine heart in the party brought home a more or less deep wound inflicted by her killing glances. Where will you find a daintier or prettier wood-nymph than our widow of the mountains? A modern Diana galloping through the fern on Jinks with her gun in her belt. To be remembered too is our "Swell Lunch" with its sixteen courses, as scored by Blond Hannah's oung man on our elegant hardwood bench. And the German also led with swan-like grace by the other vanity of Fowl. The Soldier methinks treat his measure with a somewhat melancholy air and someone said, was it Atchley Tinsley that Blond Hannah was the handsomest girl on the floor. The Chaperone saw all of this as through a glass darkly for the Cascades and Sunset from the Knob both in one day had proved rather a rush for one of her uncertain age and she deemed it highly expedient to utilize her comfortable chair for a long nap. Ah! those rows on the Lake, and the beauties of the Dell and the Wigwam and Lovers Retreat! And the Knob which the redheaded Preacher came near spoiling by calling it Awful!! the Cascades!!! Shades of Boy billie and Shorty Blue - I can never forget the bathing! The Prettiest Girl and Shorty Blue were the enthusiastic bathers, but Anna beat them all and scored 36 strokes. Undimmed in memory will I ever preserve the dinner scene, and again I hear the Chaperone say Please somebody go to the chicken cloaking his depravity under a smile both child-like and bland remarked casually to the trees - "You ain't talking to me". Through the whole days, particularly that on the pebbley road to the Cascades sounds in memory that refrain as insistent as the Katydids - "On the Banks of Chickamauga" sad too, was the partial drowning of Jean, and worthy of record the Soldier's presence of mind (After hints hard enough to fell a mule) when he fled to summons "female assistance". There are immunerable other Fernwood incidents I would love to recall but they would make volumes. I will leave you to treasure them with those other happenings that escaped the Chaperone's eye and ear and of which she hasn't the slightest suspicion.

As last the dreaded Monday, that was to begin the return to civilization dawned. Sadly we struck Camp and embarked for home, cheered at last by the distinguished presence of a charming newspaper man. This gentleman proved to be a most untiring and useful member of the expedition, had this not been the case, I fear he might have been regarded with unchristian feeling by the rest of the campers fresh from the City as he was with its style, its Turkish baths and its laundries, which we were not - decidedly were not.

They were now back at the Porterfield Farm.

The chaperone continues, "We made a stop at Camp Jean (where the dear girls saw the Devil) and enjoyed dinner, which was supplemented by buttermilk, apples and tomatoes, skirmished for by the nurse and Blond Hannah. The Widow and Jinks being still along, the Soldier + Chicken were still in their fresh & jovial spirits & hearty appetites. But an unexpected cloud suddenly obscured the Sun of their complaciency. The Widow and Boy Billie drew close together & presently went off for apples. There might have been a rift within the lute of the wagon's harmony had not the Boy while gallantly assisting the Widow up the hill, had a fall, forgetting to do it quite gracefully & so spoiled his chances with the agile lady. Shooting Creek was quiet and we pulled out without having experienced any exhilarating adventure. Our next stop was Camp Grouchy, principally memorable for its heat and cornpones. A stop at Blacksburg was cheered by a box of candy from the gentlemen & we began to think that civilization was not such a bad thing after all. Dinner on that last day was spread beneath umbraceous trees at Price's Forks. Mr. Hearnon brought melons by the pound even though the Groceryman refused to take back the rinds which Mr. Hearon magnamiously fed to the pigs. This was a dinner hard to forget. In neglect of such delicacies as shrimps, tomatoes and canned cherries, Mr. Chicken ate exclusively & most heartily of cornpone as chickens will. Mr. Adams slept & dreamed of a home where buttermilk and butter flow & where apples and tomatoes dare not affect his soul. In the last stage of the happy journey the Chaperone earnestly received her charges and came to the following conclusions. All but especially some were happier than when they started though sunburn & guise the light of that happiness shone. All had proved themselves unselfish, plucky & goodnatured. The Queen had revealed herself as the orderly fair of the occasion. Although Anna irretrievably laid herself open to the charge of coquetry she made amends by ably assisting the Chaperone in preventing a spread of the contagion. Jean merits a vote of thanks for having created two sensations & had also a birthday. Mary's young man being somewhere else, she was able to be a constant solace & delight to the chaperone, who found in her a kindred giggler. The nurse sound in her science, sound in her cooking but a little off in her theology, had proved herself one of the most active and useful members of the expedition. Mr. Chicken - but at his name methinks I hear him murmur "You ain't talking to me." Mr. Kurtz the young ladies pet, will ever be a cherish ed memory in connection with his oars & his long sweep of them. The two Hannah's had their "beauty been their sole duty" would have still been indisputable but they were useful as well as ornamental and last but not least the Dependable was all his name implies & much more. At last we drew up in front of Col. Kinderdines gate where we started. The Chaperone was about to disappear into the bosom of her deserted family when three loud & hearty cheers led by "Shake" startled the drowsy air. The Chaperone realizing that they were in her honor gracefully assumed the attitude known as

"Bless you my children" said "Ladies and Gentlemen I Love you all" or at least she would had she thought of it in time.

Signed, The Chaperone

(This journal is used with permission of the owner, Minnie Adams Fitting)

And so comes in a new century at Mountain Lake. Many events had occurred since Christopher Gist and his Indian guides had first looked at Mountain Lake. Joy and sadness had rested beside its waters. What would the new century bring? Hopefully it will be our good fortune to see it unfold as the records come forth to reveal its secrets.

The Kinderdine and Adams Camp
at Mountain Lake August 24, 1900
(Photo courtesy Minnie Fitting)

The Resort in 1900 welcoming the new century
(Photo courtesy Robert Farrier)

Bibliography

Adams, Radford C. Papers, "A Camping Trip to Mountain Lake" used by permission of Minnie Adams Fitting.

Barger Family Records Family papers in the possession of Lucy Lee Lancaster.

Beyer, Edward Description of the Album of Virginia or The Old Dominion Illustrated v. I (Richmond, Va.: Enquirer Book and Job Printing Office, 1857)

Boy, Herman Map of Virginia as seen in Johnson, The New River Early Settlement.

Burke, William The Mineral Springs of Virginia (Morris and Brothers,1851)

Church of Jesus Christ of Latter-Day Saints, The, Manuscript History of the Southern States Mission, Giles County Virginia and Baptismal Records of Mountain Lake Sunday School in possession of Bobby Wilburn.

Darlington, W. M. Christopher Gist's Journals with historical, geographical and ethnological notes (Cleveland: Arthur H. Clark Co, 1893)

Givens, Lula Porterfield Highlights in the Early History of Montgomery County, Virginia (Pulaski: B.D. Smith and Bros. Printers Inc., 1975)

Givens, Virginia Price A Hunt on Mountain Lake Mountain (Unpublished manuscript in Author's Collections)

Haupt, Herman Mountain Lake Brochure Advertising Mountain Lake (Philadelphia: Herman Haupt, 1889)

Hopper, Margaret and Bollinger, G.A. The Earthquake History of Virginia 1774-1900 (Blacksburg: VPI&SU, Geology Dept. 1971)

Johnson, Patricia Givens The New River Early Settlement (Pulaski: Edmonds Printing Co., 1981)

Johnson, Patricia Givens The United States Army Invades the New River Valley May 1864 (Christiansburg: Walpa Publishing, 1986)

Johnston, David E. A History of the Middle New River Settlements and Contiguous Territory (Huntington, West Virginia: By Author, 1906)

Kercheval, Samuel History of the Valley of Virginia (2d edition, 1850)

Kinzer, William L. Diary of ... (Virginia Historical Society)

Lyon, John Nurseryman and Plant Hunter and His Journal 1799-1814 ed. Joseph Ewan, Trans American Philosophical Society, v. 53.

McGraw, Samuel Survey, July 5, 1794, Montgomery County Courthouse (VPI&SU Special Collections)

Marland, F.C. The History of Mountain Lake Giles County, Virginia An Interprtation based on paleolimnology (Blacksburg: VPI&SU, 1967)

Marryat, Frederick Diary in America (Bloomington: Indiana University Press, 1960)

Martin, Joseph A New and Comprehensive Gazetteer of Virginia and the District of Columbia (Charlottesville: Mosely and Tompkins Printers,1835)

Moorman, Dr. J.J. The Virginia Springs (Philadelphia: J.B. Lippincott, 1859)

Mountain Lake Resort Brochures, 1889, 1895, 1897, 1898, 1900, 1904

Nicklin, P. H. (Peregrine Prolix) Letters Descriptive of the Virginia Springs (Philadelphia: H.S.Tanner 1839)

Nicolay, John Lewis Miller Artist "Mountainside Magazine" v. I, no.2, pp. 6-10.

Official Records of the Rebellion, v. 29, pt. 1, Series I. Operations in N.C., Va., W. Va., Pa., Md. 1863 Expeditions Against Lewisburg

Parker, Bruce C., H.E. Wolfe and R. Vincent Howard On the origin and history of Mountain Lake, Virginia Southeastern Geology, v. 16, no.4, May 1975

Pendleton, W.C. History of Tazewell County (Richmond: W.C. Hill Printing Company 1920)

Pollard, E.A. The Virginia Tourist (Philadelphia: J.B. Lippincott, 1870)

Pursch, Frederick Flora Americae Septentrionalis ed. by Joseph Ewan, American Philosophical Society v. 52.

Rachal, W.M.E. "A Trip to the Salt Pond" Virginia Cavalcade, Autumn 1952.

Richmond Daily Dispatch v. XVIII no.158, July 3, 1860.

Roanoke Times, January 31, 1938 "Evidences Remain of Yankee Foray Through Gile".

Tanner, H.S. New Map of Virginia with its Canals, Roads and Distances from place to place along the state and steamboat routes (Philadelphia: H.S. Tanner 1836)

U.S. Geological Survey Topographical Map Pearisburg Quad. 15' Series 1937

Virginia, State of,Acts of the General Assembly, 1856, Chap. 53, 193, 344.

Virginia, State Library, Board of Public Works, Mt. Lake and Salt Sulphur Springs Turnpike Bill, January 24, 1860 J.E. Alexander to Thomas DeWitt 1860. Williams, Charles R. ed.,

Diary and Letters of Rutherford B. Hayes 19th President of the United States v.2, 1861-65 (New York: Kraus Reprint Company, 1971).

Williams, R.L. Mountain Lake Hotel (unpublished MMS. Special Collections VPI&SU)

Letters and Interviews:

Interviews

Author with Dr. Wallace Lowry, Geology Dept. VPI&SU, Sept.1987.

Author with Dr. G.A. Bollinger, Geology Dept. VPI&SU, Sept.1987.

Author with Ward and Alice Williams, Sept. 1987.

Author with Martha Ellison Hesser, 1985-1987.

Author with Dorothy Meredith Akers, Oct. 15, 1984.

Author with Hugh P. Givens and Charles Atkins, 1939.

Author with Robert Farrier grandson of Gordon Porterfield, 1986.

Letters

Tinsley, Charles F. Hoges Store, Virginia to Bierne Ellison August 27, 1895 in Author's Collections.

Ewan, Nesta New Orleans, La. to Lee Pendleton, May 16, 1967 in Author's Collections.

Porterfield, T. Gilbert to Lula Porterfield Givens, Feb. 13, Mar. 1, Mar. 9, 1963 in Author's Collections.

Franklin, Hobert to Author, Aug. 24, Sept. 4, 1987.